Report Writing

Report Writing

A Survival Guide

Joyce Kupsh and Rhonda Rhodes

Library of Congress Control Number:		2010906992
ISBN:	Hardcover	978-1-4500-6893-2
	Softcover	978-1-4500-6892-5
	eBook	978-1-4500-6894-9

This book was printed in the United States of America.

Second Edition

To order additional copies of this book, contact:
Xlibris
1-888-795-4274
www.Xlibris.com
Orders@Xlibris.com
585355

Contents

Acknowledgements 11

Introduction.. 13

Chapter 1   Organizing 17

    Purposes 18
        Inform.. 18
        Interpret... 18
        Recommend.. 19
        Persuade... 19
    Types of Reports... 20
        Research Report 20
        Case Study Analysis 20
        Case Study 21
        Feasibility Study 22
        Strategic Plan.. 22
        Business Plan 23
        Business Proposal.. 23
        Evaluation Report 24
        Synthesis Report 24
        Assessment/Audit Report 24
        Technical Report.. 24
        Follow-up Report 24
        Press Release 24
        Miscellaneous 25

Format Styles 25
    E-mail, Memo, Letter 25
    Form 26
    Report.. 26
    Newsletter.. 27
    Brochure... 27
    Magazine, Booklet, or Manual 28
    Social Media 29
Parts of a Report.................................... 31
    Executive Summary/Abstract 31
    Contents 32
    Introduction... 33
    Body.. 33
    Bibliography/References/Resources.......... 34
    Appendices 34

Chapter 2   Starting 37

Planning.. 38
    Purposes or Objectives........................... 38
    Target Audience 39
    Time Schedule 39
    Overall Plan.. 40
Researching 41
    Secondary Data 41
    Primary Data....................................... 41
Outlining... 42
    Preparation 42
    Evaluation 43

Chapter 3   Referencing 45

Quotations.. 47
Paraphrases 48
Summaries... 48
Reference Management Software 49
    Reference Checkers............................ 51
    Citation Creators 51
Citing Sources 51
    Parenthetical................................... 51
    Endnotes 52
    Footnotes 52
Using Style Manuals 53
APA Reference List................................... 53
Avoiding Plagiarism 54

Chapter 4   Writing 59

Objectivity 60
Conciseness 61
    Irrelevant Information.......................... 61
    Redundancy 61
    Clutter and Clichés............................ 62
    Extra Phrases 62
    Implied Ideas 63
    Abstract or General Words...................... 63
Coherence.. 64
    Repetition 64
    Transition 64
Tone... 66
    Positive versus Negative 66
    Active versus Passive 67
    Expletives 67
    Pronouns...................................... 67
    Bias-Free Language............................ 68

Emphasis 69
Variety 69
Comprehensive 70

Chapter 5   Polishing 73

Abbreviations 74
Acronyms 74
Capitalization 75
Italics 77
Numbers 77
Punctuation 79
    Apostrophe 79
    Colon 79
    Comma 80
    Dash 80
    Diagonal 81
    Ellipsis 81
    Exclamation Point 81
    Hyphen 81
    Parentheses 82
    Period 82
    Question Mark 82
    Quotation Marks 82
    Semicolon 83
Spelling 83
Word Division 85

Chapter 6   Producing 89

Fonts 89
    Classifications 90
    Variations 92
    Sizes 93
    Line Spacing 94
    Alignment 94

Color..95
Paper 95
    Type 96
    Weight 96
    Size..96
Layout 96
    Page Orientation 97
    Margins 97
    Column Size...97
    Blank Space..98
    Headings and Subheadings 98
    Page Numbers 99
    Headers and Footers..............................99
    Binding 100
    Cover 100
Graphics..100

Chapter 7   Finishing..................................105

Editing...106
    Substance..106
    Style 106
    Consistency 107
Proofreading 107
    Techniques 107
    Tips 108

Checklists 111

Index..131

Acknowledgements

We truly appreciate the suggestions and comments from our reviewers:

Dr. Nancy Merlino
College of Agriculture
California State Polytechnic University, Pomona

Leanne Powers
College of Business Administration
California State Polytechnic University, Pomona

Dr. Harry Smallenberg
Pasadena Community College

Andi Gray
K and A General Contracting
Cornville, Arizona

Graduate and Undergraduate Students
California State Polytechnic University
Pomona, California

A special thank you goes to Joe Cruz for the artwork.

Joyce Kupsh – jkupsh@cox.net

Rhonda Rhodes – rrhodes@csupomona.edu

Introduction

> *2day, much of r communication is by txts. U no how 2 txt. U txt all the time 2 yr BFFs. OMG u LOL & give TMI. U tweet with Twitter & post on Facebook. BTW, u email, chat, & IM, & these methods wrk gr8 4 u.*
>
> **—Rhodes and Kupsh**

Many methods of communicating are used in the twenty-first century. Telephones, letters, reports, and faxes are still used; but now we use text messaging, instant messaging, e-mail, voice mail, Facebook, and Twitter. These new methods have a language entirely different from the established communication language of the working world.

However, in order to succeed in college, on the job, and in life, you must be able to produce a top-notch report. Effective reports are planned, researched, outlined, referenced, and formatted for their particular purpose and audience. A report can be one page or numerous pages. But all reports should include correct grammar, punctuation, and spelling, as well as objectivity, conciseness, thoroughness, coherence, and an eye-catching format. You must be aware of the types, format choices, and the parts of a report.

Report Writing—A Survival Guide will help you with the foundation of producing an effective report. Whether you are writing a case study, a research report, or a strategic plan, the **Checklists** at the end of the book will help ensure your written communication is successful for its intended purpose. The material appears in an orderly arrangement. However, you may choose to refer to a particular section as needed.

Chapter 1

Organizing

> *Organize, organize, organize! Organization is absolutely critical to successful communication. Before you actually write a word, you should spend time thinking and arranging. You must consider the purpose, type, format, style, and parts of your report.*
>
> **—Rhodes and Kupsh**

Organizing means to arrange or order things so that they can be found or used easily and quickly, according to Merriam Webster Dictionary.

The time you spend thinking and arranging—organizing—will payoff throughout the completion of your report. When organizing a report, you need to think about the

- **Purpose** of the report
- **Type** of report that works best
- **Format** that will be the most effective.

Purposes

All reports are written for a reason. The reason may be to inform, interpret, recommend, persuade, or some combination of these reasons.

Inform

Written communications that inform may tell the status or progress of a situation. Social media is a popular means of informing in today's technology world. Examples of social media are Facebook, which informs friends of our status, LinkedIn, which is used by people in the business world, or Twitter, which shares an opinion in 144 characters or less. Even though the various types of social media inform, they require special care in their organization and writing of reports.

Examples of various types of reports that inform are as follows:

- *Company annual report*—tells the shareholders the status of the company.
- *Sales report*—provides the sales performance for a week/ month/year.
- *Construction report*—updates the progress a company has made toward completion of the new company headquarters.
- *Procedures*—includes procedures to be followed.
- *Documentation*—describes occurrences or events.
- *Financial reports*—includes such things as income and expense statement, balance sheet, credit standing showing financial position
- *Facebook*—informs our friends of our personal business and status.
- *Twitter*—informs in 144 characters or less one's opinion.
- *LinkedIn*—informs about jobs, productivity, and other business concerns.

Interpret

Rather than simply stating the condition, interpretive reports advance to a higher level, going beyond the facts and including an analysis or interpretation of the facts. Examples of this type of report are:

- *Sales or marketing reports*—analyzes the reasons for an increase or decrease in a given period of time.
- *Research and development report*—describes the performance standards of a new product.
- *Scientific or technical reports*—investigates numerous activities.
- *Financial reports*—explains the budget needs for a new venture.

Recommend

Reports may include information and provide an interpretive analysis and then go to the next step of providing solutions or recommendations. Any of the reports listed under the previous category may include a recommendation. Other examples are the following:

- *Case studies, business proposals, and many other types of reports*—includes facts and ends with recommendations.
- *Theses or dissertations*—investigates a topic by conducting original research—such as a survey, a series of interviews, an experimental study—and analyzes the results, and providing recommendations for the future.
- *Investigation and analysis of a product or company*—including one or more recommendations of how improvements can be made.

Persuade

Reports may be written in an attempt to persuade or generate action of some type. A persuasive report might contain elements of all three previous types of reports—inform, interpret, and recommend—but then go one more step and add an emotional appeal to the recommendation. Examples are as follows:

- *Sales proposals*—soliciting new business from clients.
- *Requests*—suggesting a change of some type.
- *Solicitation of funds*—requesting funds for a given task or activity.

Types of Reports

Many types of reports are required today. Yet, reports in general have commonalities and similar requirements. The information provided in this book applies to any type of report. However, your report may fall into one of the following types.

Research Report

A research report is routinely assigned in schools and universities. This type of report addresses a particular problem or topic and can include material found in existing scholarly journals, magazines, newspapers, books, Web sites, as well as original research.

Research Report Components
Introduction and topic, issue, or problem statement
Review of relevant existing sources
Original data
Findings
Summary, conclusions, and recommendations
Bibliography, References, and Resources

Case Study Analysis

Numerous college classes use case study analysis as part of the learning process. An effective case study analysis can vary but usually includes the following components.

Case Study Analysis
Investigate and analyze the company's history and growth.
SWOT—strengths, weaknesses, opportunities, threats
Analysis of the competition and the whole external environment
Corporate-level strategy and issues
Business-level strategy and issues
Identify possible strategic actions
Recommend actions supported by the findings
Bibliography, References, and Resources

Case Study

A case study is a report that allows you to present a product, service, or solution to a prospective client. A case study should be written with a specific goal or client in mind.

Case Study
Company profile
Business situation
Technical situation
Issues of importance
Proposed solution
Benefits
Products and services
Recommendations that are supported by the findings
Bibliography, References, and Resources

Feasibility Study

A feasibility study evaluates the desirability and practicality (feasibility) of a project, product, or decision. Before time and money are invested, businesses need to know the likelihood for success of the project.

Feasibility Study Components
Introduction to the project, product, or decision being investigated
Discussion of evaluation tools and methods
Presentation of findings
Discussion of feasibility
Recommendations
Bibliography, References, and Resources

Strategic Plan

Strategic, tactical, and operational plans are included in this formal document that presents goals, means for achieving these goals, and calendars detailing when each goal will be achieved. Strategic, tactical, and operational plans present current management's recommended actions for the foreseeable future as well as a mission and vision.

Strategic Plan Components
Environmental Analysis—profiles of present and forecasted environments
Competitive Analysis—SWOT—Include all competitors
Mission—your organization's purpose today
Vision—your organization's purpose in the future
Strategic Plans—grand strategies including how, when, and costs
Strategic Objectives—link mission to vision: financial, customer, operational
Tactical Plans—long-range goals stating how, when, and costs
Operational Plans—short-range goals stating how, when, and costs

Evaluation—measures, monitors, and tracks whether you are achieving your strategic plan
Control—describes how you will make changes
Bibliography, References, and Resources

Business Plan

The goal of a business plan is to persuade the readers into agreeing with your ideas. Usually, you are attempting to get something, such as money, equipment, or help.

Business Plan
Executive Summary—includes the highlights of everything below
Company Description—includes history, start-up plans, uniqueness
Product or Service—describes what you are selling, focuses on benefits
Market Analysis—identifies your market and customer needs
Competitive Analysis—identifies your competitors—SWOT
Strategy and Implementation—includes dates and budgets
Management Team—identifies and describes key management members
Financial Analysis—pro forma profit and loss and cash flow
Bibliography, References, and Resources

Business Proposal

A proposal is usually created in response to a request for proposal (RFP). The proposal should include all topics listed in the RFP and present your offer in the best light as well as outline what you are offering. A good business proposal will persuade someone to accept your offer and will protect you by defining exactly what actions you will take.

Evaluation Report

An evaluation report is a systematic and impartial examination of actions or processes within an organization. This type of report does not make recommendations for change; it just states what is happening at the time of the report.

Synthesis Report

A synthesis report is an analysis of a series of evaluation reports to form an overall picture and assessment of the projects, policies, or programs that have been evaluated.

Assessment/Audit Report

An assessment report can be internal or external. Included in the assessment are internal reviews, impact assessments, monitoring activities, policy reviews, and operational research. Audit reports focus on what improvements can be made. These reports are written as factual and nonjudgmental.

Technical Report

A technical report provides needed information clearly and in an easy-to-read format. Technical reports focus on solutions to problems, not on the problems.

Follow-up Report

After the implementation of a new policy or project, procedure, hardware, software, etc., the follow-up report outlines the effectiveness of what was implemented. Desired changes are also included.

Press Release

A press release announces a newsworthy item. It should include all the relevant information about the story, such as who, what, where, why, when, and how.

Miscellaneous

Other types of reports include procedure manuals, operating instructions, announcements, and documentation. All of the reports have many similarities in their format.

Format Styles

Format choices for any of the various classifications of reports will be examined next. All reports should be attractively produced in an easy-to-read format. Requirements may be even greater if a report is to recommend or persuade. The facts and figures in the report are of no value if the intended audience never reads it.

The value of a good format is that it gets the attention of the receiver and makes the task of reading easy. Formats may include e-mail, memo, letter, form, or report. However, the report can be produced with variations as a newsletter, brochure, magazine, booklet, manual, or social media.

The production techniques in Chapter 6—**Producing** apply to all of the format styles. However, some details on newsletters and brochures are included in this section.

E-mail, Memo, Letter

Many information reports need be nothing more than an e-mail or memo. The memo heading can be the company stationery provided for memos. Such stationery is intended for use in communicating with people within the office or company. In contrast, a letterhead is normally used if correspondence is with someone outside of the company.

You can save time by creating a personalized signature for an e-mail or a template for a memo. Advantages of creating a signature or template of your own can be twofold: (1) you will not need to rekey your own identification information each time you write an e-mail or memo, and (2) you can use a design or logo, including a photo or clip art, that attracts favorable notice.

An e-mail, memo, or a letter may be the appropriate vehicle for many of your reports. If the reports are longer than two or three pages, however, you may find it better to use the memo or letter for a cover message. This cover message could be kept short but is effective in introducing or explaining the attached or enclosed report.

If the contents of the report can be included in a short e-mail, memo, or letter, you can still take advantage of the production features suggested in Chapter 6—**Producing.** For instance, side headings, bold and larger font sizes, color, and graphics, can be used. Such devices make the information more attractive, resulting in easier reading or scanning.

Form

Many times a report is just completing a form. If the form is in an electronic format, you have the advantage of being able to key in the requested information.

If you cannot get an electronic copy of the form, you may want to take the time to replicate the form by scanning or keying it into your computer. Even though these tasks are time-consuming, it may be worth the effort—particularly if reporting on the same form is going to be needed again in the future.

Report

A report does not have to look like an old-fashioned manuscript. By applying the production techniques discussed in **Producing**, your report can look like a magazine article or an annual company report.

Variations are to allow more space on either the right or left side, side notes, and illustrations. The advantages of these techniques are readability. Also, blank space is available for the reader to scribble notes or make additions or corrections if desired.

Newsletter

The goal of a newsletter is to communicate information to readers. A typical newsletter is a printed report providing news to a special group.

The special group may be people within an organization; the newsletter then becomes a communication device allowing information to flow either upward to management or downward to the employees. The special interest group may be individuals outside of a company who are concerned with a special topic, such as members of a professional organization or a hobby club.

Newsletters are information reports that are published on a timely basis, such as weekly, monthly, quarterly, or yearly. A challenge in designing a newsletter is to develop a format and general identifying look and, in addition, make each particular newsletter unique.

Newsletter Tips
Develop a logo, nameplate, or flag for the title—usually on the first sheet either at the top or left edge.
Create a heading listing the editor(s) and any others responsible for the publication along with their addresses, phone numbers, etc.
Choose desired column and type sizes—if narrower columns, use a smaller type size.
Keep text readable—usually defined as seven to ten words on each line.
Add interest with graphics and art—a good idea is to break monotony by using text-wrap techniques around the art.
Choose a thickness for lines that neither overpower nor get lost.
Consider allowing space for applying a label and sending as a self-mailer without an envelope.

Brochure

A brochure is a flyer, leaflet, or small pamphlet and is used in almost every area of business and education. A common use of a brochure is an announcement appropriate for advertising a meeting or a product. However, it can also be used as a fairly brief informative report.

A well-done brochure presents a lot of information in an attractive manner. For example, a brochure may contain an announcement of a product or a meeting, educational material, or a persuasive message.

Information on a brochure can be printed on both sides of a sheet of paper. Although the paper can be any size, standard 8 ½ × 11 paper or legal 8 ½ × 14 paper are the most frequent choices. Either a portrait layout (vertical) or landscape (horizontal) layout is possible.

Brochure Tips
Be sure the information is complete—when, where, why, who, and how.
Create a masthead listing the editor(s) and any others responsible for the publication along with their addresses, phone numbers, etc.
Keep the information simple.
Include appropriate graphics and visuals to make the brochure attention getting.
Select a small font size for the body text and vary the font sizes on other text to make the important information stand out.
Make some of the information into bullet listings or enumerations, boxes, tables, etc.
Use one of the panels to make the flyer into a self-mailer so that an envelope is not needed.
Use templates from the software or purchase color designed paper and plan the brochure around the design on the paper or create your own design.
Purchase brochures pre-scored for folding or even with a business card that is perforated and can be removed by the reader.

Magazine, Booklet, or Manual

The main difference between a newsletter or brochure and a magazine, booklet, or manual is that the latter groups contain more pages. *Magazine, booklet*, or *manual* are terms used somewhat interchangeably and could be considered in the book category. In fact, the techniques mentioned under "newsletters" also apply in this category; however, the page size may be reduced to standard book sizes.

Social Media

According to the Glossary of Personal Computing, 2014, "Social media is the collective of online communications channels dedicated to community-based input, interaction, content-sharing and collaboration."

Social Media is evolving so rapidly, it is difficult to provide a completely comprehensive definition. The use of social applications and social websites are thriving. In business, social media is used to market products, promote brands, and communicate with current customers and foster new business.

Social media includes social networking, social bookmarking, social entertainment, social news, microblogging, forums, and wikis. The following chart provides examples of some of the popular social media cites and their goals.

Social Media Cites	
Facebook	The most popular free social networking website that encourages users to create profiles, upload photos and video, post and send messages to friends, family, business associates, and clients.
LinkedIn	A social networking site designed specifically for the business community. The goal of the site is for members to establish networks of professional people.
Google+	Google's social network designed to imitate the way people interact offline.
Twitter	A free microblogging service where members can post 144 character messages called tweets. Hashtags (#) are used to describe the tweet's content.
Wikipedia	A free, open content online encyclopedia created through the collaborative effort of a community of registered users. Anyone registered can create an article for publication.

CONTINUED	
Reddit	A social news website and forum where stories are socially curated and promoted by site members. Hundreds of sub-communities exist. Each has a specific topic such as technology, politics, or music. Content is voted on by other members. The goal is to get stories to the top to the top of Reddit's main page.
Pinterest	A social curation website for sharing and categorizing images found online. Description of the images are required, but the main focus of the site is visual. Clicking on a particular image takes the reader to the original source.

As with any written communication, you should use common sense and good judgment when posting on social media. Be sure to familiarize yourself with the accepted practices for the particular cite you plan to use. A few *Tips for Success with Social Media* are listed in the next chart. This list is by no means comprehensive.

Tips for Success with Social Media
Be respectful.
Don't pick fights.
Include appropriate graphics and visuals for attention-getting posts.
Contribute value-added information.
Make your first impression a good one.
Separate opinions from facts.
Don't send out invitations to play games or other timewasters.
Assume that anything you post will be seen by your future boss, current client, or potential clients.
STOP. THINK. POST. Don't post when intoxicated, tired, angry, or upset.
Check grammar and spelling before posting.
Choose the right platform and interact often.
Use analytics.

CONTINUED
Be timely about posting.
Don't try to use more cites than you can keep up with.
Build social media into your business or personal plan.
Respect intellectual property rights and copyright laws.
Be positive.

Parts of a Report

The parts of a report will vary according to its specific aims and purposes. An overview of all the various parts that can be included, along with an explanation of when and why the various parts should be used, is discussed next.

Executive Summary/Abstract

An executive summary or abstract of the report states in approximately a page or less a synopsis of the entire report. In the business world, an executive summary is extremely important. The executive summary may be read and used to judge whether the report is worth reading. On the other hand, the executive summary may be effective in helping the reader make a favorable decision before reading the rest of the report. *Consider your report successful if this happens! Possibly because of its overall look of attractiveness and efficiency, your report portrays a confidence that leads to acceptance.*

The executive summary or abstract should state the report in a nutshell—generally, it could include the purpose or objectives of the report, background, procedures or approach to the report, findings, and summary, recommendations, and conclusions.

A title page provides identification for the report. A typical title page could include information such as the following:

```
┌─────────────────────────────────────────┐
│                                           │
│              **Title**                    │
│                                           │
│          **Author or Authors**            │
│                                           │
│   *company, email address, phone number   │
│        of the author(s)*                  │
│             *if needed*                   │
│                                           │
│              **Date**                     │
│                                           │
│                                           │
│             **Purpose**                   │
│                                           │
│    *prepared for whom and why if needed*  │
│                                           │
└─────────────────────────────────────────┘
```

Appropriate graphics always adds to a cover page. For example, adding a company logo is effective when doing a case analysis.

Contents

Because *Table of Contents* is a redundancy, it can also be referred to simply as *Contents*. Any report more than three or four pages long can benefit from the inclusion of a contents page. Thus, the formats of e-mail, memos, letters, or forms would not need a contents page.

Contents should appear at the top along with the headings and subheadings and the page numbers where they appear. Worded another way, the contents page is an outline; however, Roman and Arabic numbers used in the typical outline should not be included unless they are used in the report. A reference manual may include a more detailed numbering system to help in locating a specific section.

Leaders (dots or dashes) are used to help the reader follow the text to the page numbers. Most software have an automatic way of inserting the leaders. Some programs even include a way of automatically generating the contents page. Only the page number where the topic begins is listed. The introduction is always on page 1. For example:

Introduction.................................. 1	*not*	Introduction 1-2
Related Research 4		Related Research 4-6

A contents page may include all levels of headings or may be restricted to only one or two levels. In developing a contents page, remember, the purpose is to provide an overview of what the report includes and to allow readers to locate and read only specific sections.

Introduction

An introduction tells the reader(s) the purpose and the background of the report. The introduction should not include the findings or conclusions. The introduction always starts on page 1. Any pages before the introduction, such as the title page, contents page, or list of figures are normally not numbered.

Body

The body may contain a variety of different parts to fit various situations. The generic outline presented next probably sounds similar to a term paper or thesis assignment from school, but it provides some useful guidelines for any report.

>Introduction
>Related Research
>Procedures or Methodology
>Findings
>Summary, Recommendations, and Conclusions

Appendices

An appendix (singular) or appendices (plural) contains supporting material to the report. The plural form can also be spelled appendixes. This supporting material might include longer information that may be needed for verification or backup information but might distract from the normal reading flow. Examples are listings, statistics, quotations, etc. Items in an appendix should be referred to at the appropriate place in the report as Appendix A, Appendix B, etc., and placed in the order that they were mentioned.

Bibliography/References/Resources

Although frequently used interchangeably, bibliographies, references, and resources are not exactly the same thing. A bibliography contains a list of writings on a subject. References are used to list citations made. Resources indicate where additional information on a subject can be found.

Chapter 2

Starting

> *Starting can be the hardest part. You should start by planning, researching, and outlining—steps that are all crucial in creating a high-impact report. Developing a detailed outline is critical for a successful report.*
>
> *—Rhodes and Kupsh*

The first step in a writing assignment is choosing the topic. Sometimes the topic is assigned, which brings you a step closer to getting the project underway. Always try to have a topic of interest to you. The report-writing process will be easier and more beneficial if you are interested in the topic.

After selecting the topic, the next difficulty in writing may occur. It is called writer's block. Often, this block is caused by starting to write without proper planning, researching, and outlining. These steps are most important in creating a proper foundation prior to beginning the actual writing process. If you have a detailed outline, the topics in the outline become your headings and subheadings, and you simply write something under each heading and subheading.

Planning

A plan consists of a detailed scheme or method worked out in advance for the accomplishment of an objective. The steps in forming a plan involve a systematic approach to the writing process. The steps can be divided into the following categories: analyzing the target audience, setting up a time schedule, collecting the data, and establishing an organized overall plan.

Purposes or Objectives

When considering the topic for a report, always begin by determining the purpose and/or objective of the report. Sometimes it helps to think of a writing project in terms of solving a problem. Thus, the purpose or the objective of the report is to address the problem.

Problems to be solved may include meeting a need for more information on a particular topic, an analytical look involving interpretation and/or recommendations, or a persuasive pitch to generate action. Chapter 3—**Organizing** lists examples of reports that fall into different and various classifications that tend to build one upon the other. For example, a persuasive report will no doubt include information, interpretations, and recommendations, along with persuasive arguments for accepting or rejecting those recommendations.

Actually writing the problem statement is one way of beginning. The task of writing the problem statement is helpful in keeping both the writer and all subsequent readers in focus on the reasons for creating the report.

The topic or issue, also referred to as a problem statement, should be supported by listing purpose(s) or objective(s). While a problem statement explains what, purposes or objectives explain why. If the report has more than one problem, purpose, or objective, plan to list each of these separately. Careful planning, analyzing, and organizing allow you to provide a clear and concise problem statement as well as goals for your target audience.

Report Writing—A Survival Guide

Target Audience

Because a report needs to be written for a target audience, an analysis of that target audience is necessary in the planning stage of a report. The following questions may prove helpful in completing this task.

Analysis of the Target Audience
What is the educational level of the intended audience?
How much background or technical experience do members of your intended reading audience have on the topic?
Is the report an upward, downward, or lateral communication device?
What is the age level, gender, and nationality of the majority of the readers?
Will the audience be expecting a formal or informal report?
Is the report one of many, or will it be one of a kind?
Is the report expected by the readers?
What type of action—a verbal response, a written reaction, or an interview—do you anticipate from the audience?
Are you addressing the appropriate audience?

These questions are not a complete list but are merely intended to start your thinking regarding the analysis of your target audience. An essential requirement is that you have a clear understanding of your target audience so you can focus on their needs.

Time Schedule

Creating a report takes time—frequently, far more time than anticipated. A detailed timeline should be established to estimate the time necessary to complete the project—particularly if you have a completion deadline for the report.

Establishing a timeline that involves estimating the amount of time needed for each of the different steps—as well as a breakdown of time needed for work within those steps—has several merits. First, the estimate provides a step-by-step schedule to follow. Second, it establishes projected daily or weekly goals rather than one final deadline. One bit of advice that many people find useful is to set an early deadline in order to leave extra days or even a week to take care of unforeseen problems. A simple Gantt chart shows a graphic presentation of your timeline.

Even if the intermediate deadlines are not always met, a timeline will provide an indication of where you stand. Many people find that a timeline with incentives (such as a candy bar, television, or a movie) for completion can be an effective motivational device.

#	Task	Who	Start	End	Days	October	November
	Case Analysis		10/1	11/30	61		
1	Select Partner	Me	10/1	10/5	5		
2	Choose a Company	Both	10/5	10/10	5		
3	Reference Manager	Both	10/5	10/10	5		
4	Initial Research	Both	10/10	10/20	10		
5	Outline the Case	Both	10/20	10/21	1		
6	Gather all Data	Both	10/21	10/30	9		
7	Store Reference	Both	10/20	11/25	35		
8	Write Case	Both	10/30	11/25	18		

Overall Plan

A likely procedure in testing a new product by a company would be to have a time schedule, expectations, definition of tasks, definition of acceptance levels, etc. This overall plan would serve the purpose of putting everyone on the same page with the same agenda—important to the success of the test.

Similarly, a written overall plan should be prepared for a written project to show your commitment and your plans to achieve that commitment. Such a plan may be required by your superiors; but even if it is not, it is important as a means of reiterating your goals and purposes and organizing the project.

Researching

The writer of a report seldom knows all of the information to be included. Usually, a collection of some type of data is needed. Data collection for the research report consists of a scholarly or scientific investigation or inquiry. Such research is considered to be either secondary research (also referred to as existing) or primary research (also referred to as original). This data may be gathered from a variety of sources.

Secondary Data

If someone else has already completed an investigation and has documented the information, you can use that information as secondary data in support of the points that you make. Always use proper reference techniques as addressed in Chapter 3. Secondary sources include information from scholarly journals, trade journals, books, magazines, or other publications.

Start your search for secondary data by using your library's database and article search. In addition to materials found in a library, computerized databases are a good source for locating information on a given topic. These databases are available in a number of commercial online services, such as Google scholar or Yahoo! scholar. Also, most libraries subscribe to one or more specialized data search programs. Talking to a reference librarian can save time and improve the quality of your research. *Reference management software* often will import references directly from online databases.

Primary Data

Primary data includes data that you have obtained and compiled. Methods used to compile original data include surveys, experiments, interviews, focus groups, and testing.

Surveys are conducted through written questionnaires, interviews, or observations. Experiments test one method against another. In either a survey or an experiment, a research design should be developed. A research design includes details such as sample size, sampling techniques, procedures, and statistical methods used. If you are conducting original research, a book on research design could be consulted to determine proper methodology and statistical techniques for your project.

Outlining

Outlining is a vital step in organizing a written project. Organization is the process of putting something together as an orderly, functional, and structured whole; outlining is the best means of achieving this objective.

Preparation

Before developing an outline, you may find it helpful to record random thoughts and phrases about your topic—brainstorming. The next step is to begin to cluster these random thoughts into logical groups. Many word processing programs contain an outline feature, which you may find helpful as your report progresses. However, your tablet, phone, computer, or notepad is sufficient and effective for developing an outline during the brainstorming stage.

Outline Requirements
A complete, organized list of what is to be covered in the report.
Topics and subtopics using parallel construction of words within the different levels showing a breakdown of what is to be covered.
Descriptive and functional topics and subtopics rather than attention-getting ones.
The inclusion of two or more points within each subtopic.
A parallel hierarchy of topics and subtopics.
A logical or sequential arrangement of topics and subtopics—alphabetical, by size (largest to smallest or smallest to largest), by time, etc.

If possible, involving other people may be a good way to provide more ideas and thoughts. You can do the initial brainstorming and clustering before submitting a draft to another person or persons. Or, you may want to involve others in the initial brainstorming process.

Evaluation

Creating a high-impact business report does not totally depend upon the topic. A high-impact report is one that is favorably received and generates action. To accomplish these goals, a report must be carefully and thoughtfully designed during the initial preparation stage. Remember, the longest trip can be shortened by good planning that steers you in the right direction. A well-prepared outline is the first step in the right direction.

Chapter 3

Referencing

> *Referencing a source can provide you with the words of an expert and in addition gives more authority to your writing. However, failure to reference sources properly can result in plagiarism, which is a crime similar to stealing. This section gives you a guide to the various types of referencing.*
>
> **—Kupsh and Rhodes**

Using the words and ideas of an expert adds credibility to your writing and shows that you have thoroughly researched the topic. Not only is it acceptable to use the words, ideas, and graphics of others in your writing, it is encouraged. However, you must cite the reference for each source or you are plagiarizing. Remember plagiarism is a crime similar to stealing.

People in all areas of business, education, and government are not only being fired for plagiarism, but many are paying fines or even going to jail. Plagiarism—whether it is accidental or intentional—is no longer tolerated. Anytime you use the words, ideas, or graphics of another (regardless of whether you have paraphrased the other work), you MUST cite the reference. This section provides you with practical tips about the various types of referencing, as well as methods that will help you avoid plagiarism!!

Existing sources may be integrated into your writing in three ways—*quotations*, *paraphrases*, and *summaries*.

1. *Quotations* must be exactly as they appear in the original research.
2. *Paraphrases* are restating the original source material in your own words.
3. *Summaries* require you to put the main ideas into your own words, while presenting a broad overview of the original.

All three methods require you to cite the original source. You have the flexibility of choosing any of the three; however, making use of all of them at different places in your report may be the best solution.

If the majority of your report is existing sources, the information should be paraphrased or summarized. Avoid having numerous quotations that make your report choppy and unprofessional. In general you should have a minimum of ten different references in your paper.

Quotations, paraphrases, and summaries will prove valuable to you for the following reasons.

Value of Quotations, Paraphrases, and Summaries
Allows the use of experts' words and ideas.
Gives more authority to your writing.
Adds credibility to your report.
Refers to work that sets the stage for your work.
Highlights a point with which you agree or disagree.
Focuses on a prominent material by quoting the original author.
Provides support for your ideas.
Presents examples of several points of view.
Indicates to the readers that the words are not just your ideas.

Quotations

A quotation assures your readers that you have not changed the meaning. Quotations must match the source document word for word and must be attributed to the original author. In addition, it may also appear to be more authoritative. The fact that you are quoting information should be made obvious to the reader. A good rule of thumb is if you use *Copy* and *Paste* at any time, you *must* indicate that the text is a *quotation* by using quotation marks.

Quotations of 5 lines or more than 40 words should be set as a block quotation or set in from both margins by approximately 5 spaces or half an inch. When this is done, quotation marks are not used at the beginning or the end, though they may be necessary for some internal passages. (Refer to Avoiding Plagiarism at the end of this Chapter.)

Also, the insertion of personal comments and the indication of an omission are both possible in quotations. In a quotation, you may insert your comments between brackets.

Omissions from quotations are indicated by using ellipsis points—a series of three periods (...). If the ellipsis occurs at the end of the sentence, you need to use an additional point for the ending of the sentence—or four periods.

As previously noted, a quotation of less than 5 lines or 40 words can be included in the text by using quotation marks to distinguish it from your writing. If a quotation is more than a page or so in length, use only the most relevant portion or put material in summary form. Another alternative is to simply refer to the quote in the text of the report and include it as an appendix. Conversely, anything included in the appendix should be mentioned in the report at the appropriate place.

Paraphrases

Paraphrasing is restating another author's words or ideas in your own words. Paraphrasing passages rather than quoting passages may tie the work in better with your writing and also take less space.

Guidelines for Paraphrasing
The majority of material from other sources should be paraphrased or summarized.
Paraphrasing includes reading someone else's ideas and restating them in your own owns.
The paraphrased material is usually shorter than the original passage.
The ideas are still the author's, who wrote the words, and you must cite the reference or you are plagiarizing.

Even though *quotation* marks are not used when *paraphrasing*, a reader should always be able to tell exactly what is *paraphrased* and what are your own words and ideas. Statements that help when *paraphrasing* are as follows:

> According to Kupsh & Rhodes (2014)
> Kupsh & Rhodes (2014) state that . .
> Rhodes (2014) found that . .

Summaries

When only the main, overall ideas from a particular source are needed, use a summary. *Summaries* present an abbreviated edition of the source's main ideas in your words. *Summaries* include stating only the main ideas of the source in your own words.

Guidelines for Summarizing
The majority of material from other sources should be summarized or paraphrased.
Paraphrasing includes reading someone else's ideas and putting them into your own words.
A summary can be as short as a few sentences or longer, depending on the difficulty of the source material and the degree of detail you wish to present in your report.
The ideas are still the author's, who wrote the words, and you must cite the reference or you are plagiarizing.

Reference Management Software

Reference management software is used for recording and citing bibliographic references. Once you store a citation, it can be used over and over when creating citations or bibliographies. Reference management software is also called *citation management software* or *personal bibliographic management software*.

These software packages usually consist of a database where bibliographic references are entered and stored, plus a system for generating selective lists of articles in different formats, such as APA, MLA, etc. Many reference management packages can be integrated into your word processing software so citations and a reference list in the appropriate format is produced automatically as a report is written, reducing the risk that a cited source is not included in the reference list. In addition to managing references, most *reference management software* also enables users to search references from online libraries.

Reference Management Software		
Software	*Cost*	*Features*
Aigaion	Free	Web-based, annotated, organized by topics
BibBase	Free	Centrally-hosted website, intended for scientific publication

BibDesk	Free	BibTeX front-end + repository, Mac
Bookends	$99	Integrated web search, pdf download, auto-completion
Docear	Free	Java BibTeXmanager that integrates Mind mapping software
EndNote Basic	Free	Web version
Mendeley	Free Online Storage	Desktop & Web, Windows, Linux, OS X, iPhone & iPad
Paperpile	$3/Month Academics, $10/Month	Web-application, integrates with Google Docs, collaborate & share, only on Google Chrome
Qiqqa	Free and Premium	Desktop; Tablet; Web; Intranet
ReadCube	Free	Desktop,Web, Mobile components, integrated web search, enhanced PDF
refbase	Free	Web-based for institutional repositories/ self-archiving
Referencer	Free	BibTeX front-end
Wikindx	Free	Web-based
WizFolio	$25 & Free Version	Centrally-hosted website
Zotero	Free Storage Free 300 MB	Firefox, Chrome and Safari. Web-based access to reference library.

One advantage of reference management software is the time users save inserting formatted citations into academic work. However, each user or group has to develop their own personal database of references. This process can itself be time consuming. Possible alternatives to reference management software are citation creators and reference checkers.

Reference Checkers. When using reference checkers you do not have to develop and maintain your own database of references. Reference checkers take completed or almost completed reports and compare the citations listed in the report with the references listed in the bibliography or references at the end. Inconsistencies between the citations and the reference list are then highlighted. Reference checkers claim to save you time because you don't have to compare your citations to your reference list. However, you must create and format the citations and the reference page.

Citation Creators. Citation creators or citation generators use online web forms to format citations and bibliographies according to specific style manuals such as APA—American Psychological Association, MLA—Modern Language Association, Chicago Manual of Style, and others. Some citation creators do not allow you to store any information while others store the citation data for later use.

Citing Sources

A variety of methods for citing sources is available. Three general methods are *parenthetical, endnotes, and footnotes*. While parenthetical is commonly used and easy for the reader, always consider your intended audience and any specific guidelines when choosing a method for citing sources. If a specific style is required, see the section Style Guides for more information. By reading your citation, the reader should be able to easily locate the exact original resource.

Parenthetical

Parenthetical references provide the advantages of footnotes and endnotes. They are easy for the writer to use and provide adequate, convenient citations within the text for the reader. In fact, this method is probably the easiest and also the most convenient for the reader.

In parenthetical references, a shortened reference is placed in parentheses within the text. A complete listing of these sources is then placed at the end of the section, chapter, or report.

In using parenthetical references, place the last name of the author(s) and the date of publication in parentheses— separated by a comma. The name of a corporation, the name of a work, or some other means of identification may also be used with the date. The complete reference would be included in the reference page.

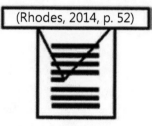

(Rhodes, 2014, p. 52)

If the author's name is mentioned in the text, then you need use only the date in parentheses. If you refer to both the author and the date in the text, nothing needs to be put in parentheses; however, the reference should still be included in the alphabetical listing at the end of the report. If the quote is from a specific page, you should include the page number in case a reader wants to locate the original writing.

Endnotes

Endnotes are indicated in the text by a raised number, though some systems may use a number in parenthesis on the same line as the text. The endnote eliminates the need for footnotes at the bottom of the page. Instead, a complete listing of the sources in numerical order is included at the end of the report along with an alphabetized list of those same references. This method requires two lists but eliminates footnotes at the bottom of a page. The reader must turn to the back of the report to identify the sources.

Footnotes

Footnotes are made by placing a raised number in the text at the end of the quotation—either direct, paraphrased, or summaries. Identification is then placed at the bottom of the page under a one-inch line. In order to identify a source, the reader must look at the bottom of the page.

[1]Graves, p. 52.

Using Style Manuals

Numerous reference styles are available depending upon your need. A more formal style is needed for collegiate writing, while a less technical approach is probably adequate for business and other needs. American Psychological Association (APA) publication manual is the most commonly used in business.

Five popular style manuals are listed in the chart. For more details on each of these styles, you can search the Web. A number of Web sites are available to provide details on how to cite various types of references. If you have specialized material to reference and cannot find an example, try to establish some logical arrangement. Remember to use common sense and to be consistent.

Popular Style Guides or Manuals
American Psychological Association (APA) Publication Manual
Form and Style: Research Papers, Reports, and Theses by Slade, Campbell, and Ballou
The Chicago Manual of Style
MLA Handbook for Writers of Research Papers by Gibaldi and Achtert
A Manual for Writers of Term Papers, Theses and Dissertations by Turabian

APA Reference List

APA style requires you to provide a reference list at the end of your paper. The list should be double spaced, and each line after the first one in each entry should be indented. The title of the list should be "References" and should be centered at the top of the page. The entire list should be alphabetized by either the author's last name or the first word of the reference. When two works by the same author are listed, order the references by date of publication.

Avoiding Plagiarism

Written communication skills are valued in every profession, from a teacher to a business executive to a nurse. This fact has caused schools to incorporate writing assignments in almost every class. However, plagiarism is an epidemic in schools and in industry. In schools, students are suspended and faculties are fired for plagiarizing. On the job, employees may be demoted or fired for any type of plagiarism. Most schools and universities have a policy like the following:

> Plagiarism, is falsification or fabrication, it is presenting words, ideas or work of others as one's own work. Plagiarism includes, but is not limited to: copying homework, copying lab reports, copying computer programs, using a work or portion of a work written or created by another but not crediting the source, using one's own work completed in a previous class for credit in another class without permission, paraphrasing another's work without giving credit, and borrowing or using ideas without giving credit (Cal Poly Pomona, University Catalog 2014-2015, *http://catalog.csupomona.edu/content. php?catoid=7&navoid=1012#Academic_Integrity*).

> Disciplinary outcomes related to plagiarism may include, but are not limited to: warnings, probation, suspension, expulsion, or educational assignments intended to discourage the recurrence of academic dishonesty. (Cal Poly Pomona, University Catalog 2014-2015, *http://catalog.csupomona.edu/content. php?catoid=7&navoid=1012#Academic_Integrity*).

Guidelines for Avoiding Plagiarism
If you use the *exact words* of an author, put the words in quotation marks and cite the reference.
If you use the *ideas* of another, even if you change the words around, you must cite the reference. The ideas are not yours.
If you *paraphrase* or *summarize* material from another source, you must cite the reference.

Do not *buy* or *borrow* a paper from a Web site, classmate, or a friend. You are plagiarizing and committing fraud.
Do not use a *paper you wrote for a previous class* in your current class, without getting permission or recognizing the previous use. Otherwise, you are plagiarizing.
Plan ahead and start your report early. Proper referencing of sources takes time. Effective writing takes time. Don't get in a desperate situation and say, "They probably won't catch it if I copy this."
Keep track of your sources; print electronics sources.
Keep sources in correct context.
Don't cut and paste; file and label your sources.
Keep your own writing and your sources separate.
Keep your notes and your draft separate.
Paraphrase carefully in your notes; acknowledge yours sources explicitly when paraphrasing or summarizing.
Avoid reading a classmate's paper for inspiration.
Don't save your citations for later.
Quote your sources properly.

Giving students a Web-based tutorial on plagiarism is more effective in deterring the behavior than threatening students with detection and punishment. That's according to the results of an experiment conducted by professors at the University of Michigan and Swarthmore College . . . . The study, *Rational Ignorance in Education: A Field Experiment in Student Plagiarism*, found that incidents of plagiarism could be reduced by as much as 65 percent when students participated in a 15-minute Web-based tutorial that [taught them] what constitutes plagiarism and how to avoid it. (Nagel, *Campus Technology*, 2010)

The copy-and-paste features are valuable when writing reports. However, when you copy someone's words or ideas and then paste them into your report, it is sometimes difficult to find the source later. It is better to file, label, and print each source as it is found. Always write the source on any material you collect. It is very frustrating to have a perfect quote that you cannot use because you are unable to locate the source. *Reference management software* is a great tool for organizing and citing your sources.

Don't plagiarize—it isn't worth it. You can use the words and ideas of another person, but just say whose words or ideas they are with a proper reference. Some teachers run random sentences from all reports through one of the online plagiarism Web sites. Businesses and schools alike are taking plagiarism seriously.

Chapter 4

Writing

> *Anyone can write a report. The key is to write a report that people want to read. Developing an effective writing style requires knowledge and practice. This section provides an overview of the writing style techniques that are most helpful.*
>
> *—Kupsh and Rhodes*

W riting style refers to the way ideas are expressed on the written page. Style can vary from one individual to another, reflecting the personality of the writer. Also, writing style can vary to fit a specific need or purpose.

With practice, you can improve your writing style. Consider how professional athletes practice to maintain and increase their skills. Writing is no different. Study and practice will lead to improved performance.

This section highlights the key techniques needed in developing a good style. The following techniques are discussed: objectivity, conciseness, coherence, tone, emphasis, variety, and readability. Numerous report-writing books are available if more detail is desired. Remember, this is a survival guide.

Objectivity

Reports should be written from an objective standpoint. A report does not reflect personal emotions and opinions. Instead, a report includes facts and findings that ultimately lead to recommendations and conclusions formed on the basis of those facts and findings.

You can maintain an objective attitude by divorcing yourself from your personal biases and prejudices. You should look at all sides of the problem with an open mind before stating your conclusions. This role is similar to that of a referee at a sporting event or a judge presiding in court. Decisions are based on the results, the evidence, or an interpretation of the results and evidence—not on personal opinions and feelings.

Keeping an open mind when writing will make your conclusions and recommendations more believable. If a personal bias is revealed, the reader may question the accuracy of the report. The emphasis, therefore, should be on the factual material presented and the conclusions drawn rather than on any personal beliefs.

Objective writing is impersonal and does *not* use pronouns such as *me, my, us,* or *you.* Objective writing uses names (proper nouns) and may occasionally use *he, him, she, her, they,* and *them.*

Objective writing does not mean boring or dull writing. Most newspaper and magazine articles are written objectively. While some of them may be exciting and interesting, others may lack luster, depending as much upon the subject as the writing style. Thus, even the blandest of topics can be positively affected through a blend of *what you say* (content) and *how you say it* (written expression of ideas).

At times, of course, you may want to make your writing more personal. If the report is a personal communication between you and your associates, for example, you may prefer the more informal approach of using *I, my, me, we, our, us,* and *you.* Overuse of these pronouns, however, may make you sound conceited. Thus, you may want to limit personalization.

Before you start to write, decide which style—personal or impersonal—is best for the situation. Deciding at the outset on which style is appropriate can save considerable time and effort during the editing process.

Conciseness

"More is not always better, sometimes it is just more."
(*Sabrina*, screenplay adapted by Barbara Benedek and David Rayfiel, 1995)

Conciseness is a necessity in today's busy world; it saves time and money for both the writer and the reader(s). Long reports do not necessarily equal quality reports. Important details can be lost. Teachers may do a disfavor by assigning their students a ten-page report when the information could be adequately stated in one or two pages.

The art of being concise is difficult. Conciseness is achieved in many different ways. General categories of things to avoid in making your writing more concise follow.

Irrelevant Information

Information that is irrelevant to the report should not be included. Perhaps the reader does not need to know everything you know on the subject. Everything included in the report should be there for a reason and have a bearing on your topic and your purpose. A detailed outline helps eliminate irrelevant information.

Redundancy

Redundancy is the useless repetition of a word. Eliminate redundancy from your reports. Examples of redundancies are illustrated in the following list.

> 6 p.m. ~~in the afternoon~~
> ~~free~~ gifts
> ~~important~~ essentials
> ~~basic~~ fundamentals
> ~~personal~~ opinion

~~falsely~~ padded expense account

~~severe~~ crisis

she ~~is a female who~~

Clutter and Clichés

Clutter and clichés are frequently combined in a way that wastes words. The following examples demonstrate ways of making writing more concise.

~~will you please arrange to send~~	please send
~~a check in the amount of~~	a check for
~~in accordance with your request~~	as requested
~~we are not in a position to~~	we cannot
~~reports that are long~~	long reports

Extra Phrases

Using hyphenated words (compound adjectives) help reduce the number of words needed to express an idea.

~~The writing techniques which are up to date~~
Up-to-date writing techniques

~~Reports written at the last minute~~
Last-minute reports

~~Avoid waiting until the last minute~~
Avoid the last-minute rush

Substituting a precise word or words for phrases eliminates extra words.

~~Tom was a teacher who was outstanding.~~
Tom was an outstanding teacher.

~~Writers create better output when they use a production package.~~
Writers using a production package create better output.

~~The report which is incomplete~~
The incomplete report

~~Paul waited in an impatient manner.~~
Paul waited impatiently.

Implied Ideas

Implied (obvious) ideas need not be restated. The following statements can be rewritten omitting words as shown.

~~She went to school and attended class,~~
She attended class,

~~He took the test and passed it with high honors.~~
He passed the test with high honors.

~~Mary went shopping and bought a~~
Mary bought a

Abstract or General Words

On the other hand, using a single concrete word rather than a longer phrase will shorten the sentence but make the meaning somewhat vague. In reporting on the work ability of a person, words such as *dependable, efficient, nice,* and *superior* may sound good but tend to be hazy compared to more concrete descriptive words or sentences. For instance, you could cite specific examples for each of these words.

~~dependable~~	was never late to work
	was never sick
~~efficient~~	made deadlines
	won employee-of-the-month award
~~nice~~	gets along well with all employees
~~superior~~	made the highest score in a class of two hundred

Coherence

Coherent writing flows along without abrupt changes; or to put it another way, the writing sticks together. This cohesion is accomplished by linking the thought from one sentence to the next and from one paragraph to the next. Linking is done by repeating words and by using a transition.

Repetition

By repeating a word either directly or with a similar word, you will keep the reader aware of the topic. In the following examples, the addition of the word inserted in parentheses makes the writing stronger and clarifies the meaning. Without the inserted noun, the reader might be forced to reread the previous sentence to clarify what *this, that, these,* and *those* refer to or represent.

> This *(example)* will show
> That *(task)* is accomplished
> These *(papers)* will be delivered
> Those *(plans)* are the ones

Transition

Using transitions help to blend one thought with another, keeping the reader focused on the flow of the report. Transitions help the writing flow smoothly and bridge any gaps. Transitional words include explanation, enumeration or listing, similarity or contrast, and cause or effect.

Explanation. A transition is useful before giving an example. You can use such words as the following:

also	for instance
too	to illustrate
for example	in the illustration
as an example	as previously stated

Bullet Lists. A transition is useful before writing a list of items. You can list items using a numbered list. However, many times the number is not important, and the items can be listed using a symbol such as

✓ ◆ ◆ ◻ ◯ ● ❖ ◼ ◻ ◻ ◆

Thousands of symbols are available online, or you can use a photo to create a custom symbol for your report.

If the items are short or special emphasis is not needed, you may prefer to list the items within the paragraph. This listing can be done by using the numbers: (1) first, (2) second, or (3) third. A semicolon should be used instead of a comma if the words in the listing include longer phrases using a comma.

Words within the paragraph are also effective in linking items. Examples are as follows:

in addition	third
first	next
second	finally

Similarity or Contrast. Transition words work effectively in showing either a similarity or a contrast between two situations. Some helpful examples are the following:

Similarity	*Contrast*
likewise	in contrast
similarly	in spite of
in a similar manner	on the other hand
by the same token	however
in the same way	on the contrary

Cause or Effect. Transitional words are also helpful in showing a cause or an effect:

because of	as a result
therefore	for this reason
thus	consequently

Tone

The tone of a report can convey a message to the reader(s). Care needs to be taken to assure that the right tone is projected. A neutral, unbiased stance is most convincing. Many different factors contribute to the tone of a message, such as using positive versus negative and active versus passive as well as bias-free language.

Positive versus Negative

People like to hear good news; therefore, you want to accentuate the positive and eliminate the negative aspect as much as possible. Exceptions can be made if you are consciously trying to dramatize a negative problem, but carefully analyze the negative statements to ensure that you are making the desired impression.

Some words automatically project a negative feeling or image. For instance, the words *delay, unable, cannot, inconvenient, disappointed, broken, not,* and *unfortunately* all create an *"oh dear, bad news"* effect.

If, on the other hand, you want to give a positive spin to bad news, use a more positive word.

Negative	*Positive*
~~do not forget~~	remember
~~you neglected to send~~	please send
~~not honest~~	dishonest
~~cannot accept~~	unacceptable in present form

Active versus Passive

Writing in active voice—with the subject doing the acting—is usually a direct and dynamic method of writing. Yet, passive writing may be more appropriate at times. *(See the next section on emphasis.)* Here are examples of active and passive writing:

Active	John wrote the report.
Passive	The report was written by John.

Expletives

Expletives such as *there are, it is, it is noted that, it is understood that*, etc., should be avoided. Expletives are meaningless words used in beginning a sentence. Even though a sentence with an expletive may be grammatically correct, the sentence is unclear and may cause the reader to look back in an effort to find to what the expletive refers. The following words may create interest in a novel but should be avoided in report writing.

Vague	*Definite*
~~there are~~	The report states . . .
~~it is said that~~	The research suggests . . .
~~it is understood that~~	The review indicates . . .
~~it is noted that~~	Furthermore, the results indicate . . .

Pronouns

Using a noun or the pronouns *he, she, him, her, they,* and *them* (writing in third person) is recommended for report writing. Using the pronouns *I, we, me, my, our, us,* and *them* (writing in first person) may seem to make writing more personalized, but readers may begin to think you are conceited after hearing words such as *I* or *we* too many times. Using *you* (writing in second person) is recommended for letter writing in an attempt to get the attention and interest of the reader.

You should carefully consider the desired impact *before* you start writing. Since a report is a factual account or summation of information, third-person writing may make the final result seem more businesslike.

Bias-Free Language

The tone of your writing should never reflect a gender bias or any other type of bias—race, religion, age, disability, or ethnic group. Biased writing sends the wrong message and may alienate readers.

Stereotyping. If you refer to a man as a boss and a woman as a housekeeper, you are stereotyping. Avoid stereotyping by changing to plural form when possible and referring to both genders. Problems and suggested corrections are as follows:

> ~~The manager showed his appreciation~~
> The manager showed appreciation
>
> ~~The housekeeper is required to do her best.~~
> All housekeepers are required to do their best.
>
> ~~He is to report to~~
> He or she is to report to

Job Titles. Job titles and expressions can show gender bias. Eliminate the use of biased titles and substitute a more neutral word. Most words can be stated in a more acceptable version. For instance:

~~policeman~~	police officer
~~fireman~~	firefighter
~~businessman~~	businessperson
~~working mother~~	working parent
~~foreman~~	supervisor
~~bag boy~~	bag person
~~stock boy~~	stock clerk
~~airline hostess~~	flight attendant

Emphasis

Words placed either first or last in a sentence receive the greatest emphasis. You should decide on your most important word or phrase and then decide whether you want that word or phrase to make an initial or a lasting impact.

In the following sentences, the attention is on Rodney in the first sentence. The second sentence places the emphasis on the report. If you want to give Rodney credit, place his name first. If the report being completed is more important, use the second sentence.

> ~~Rodney completed the report.~~
> The report was completed by Rodney.

Using either active or passive voice changes the emphasis of a sentence. For example, if you are portraying bad news, you may wish to write in a passive form to keep from sounding accusatory.

> ~~You neglected to include the data.~~
> The data was not included.

Variety

At times, writing rules seem to disagree. One rule will say to be parallel, and another rule will say to use variety. Both rules are correct, but each one has its place. The hard part is deciding when to be parallel and when to use variety.

In general, elements in a series—such as side headings, bullet lists, items in a series, or clauses—should be parallel. The following list provides examples of parallel writing as well as writing that is not parallel.

Variety is good in the length of sentences and paragraphs. Varying the length of sentences and paragraphs breaks the monotony for the reader. Too many short sentences may make the writing sound like a first-grader's report. However, long sentences and paragraphs may put the reader to sleep. A combination will provide needed variety.

Another way of making your writing more interesting is to use variety in sentence structure. Simple sentences are easy to read but should be mixed with complex or compound sentences. Also, vary the pattern and begin some sentences with a prepositional phrase such as "During the winter" or a dependent clause such as "Because of the low budget." If applied correctly, variety does lend interest to your writing.

Comprehensive

A report should be comprehensive, including all the necessary parts as mentioned in Chapter 1—**Organizing.** The person receiving the report should be left with no unanswered questions and should not have to request additional data from the writer. A detailed outline usually insures that all the necessary topics have been included. The **Checklists** at the end of the book provide a way to evaluate your report.

Chapter 5

Polishing

> **Polishing makes your report professional. The material included was selected after analyzing common problems made by graduate and undergraduate students in the authors' classes.**
>
> **—Kupsh and Rhodes**

The image reflected by your work will influence your readers' reaction. Your report will be regarded as flawed and viewed with skepticism if it contains numerous writing errors—even if the report has a wealth of technical, scientific, and creative information.

Many people say they are interested in only the content of a report—not how it looks or how well written it is! However, when faced with a stack of reports, all people are drawn to the reports that stand out. They are influenced by the appearance as much as by the facts and thoughts in the paper. Polishing your writing represents an extremely important piece of the writing puzzle.

This section cannot possibly cover all there is to know concerning writing skills. However, the basics as well as many of the more common errors made by writers will be included. Topics included are abbreviations, acronyms, capitalization, italics, numbers, punctuation, spelling, and word division.

Abbreviations

Abbreviations in a report should be used with caution. A few exceptions to this follow.

In general, the more formal a report, the fewer abbreviations should be used. The following list illustrates places where abbreviations are commonly used.

- Titles before and after names

  Dr. Cruz
  Mr. Rhodes
  Mrs. Gray
  Ms. Rivera
  Drs. Rhodes and Kupsh
  Mssrs. Smith and Young
  Mary Buck, Ph.D.
  Nancy Merlino, Ed.D.
  Heather Gray, M.D.
  Jim Scott Sr.

- Number when used with a figure

  No. 24

- Companies and organizations with abbreviations used in letterhead

  Brian and Co.

Acronyms

Acronyms—words formed from the initial letters of a name—of companies, departments, divisions, organizations, or agencies can save a lot of space in a report. Acronyms are so frequently used today that they have become an integral part of our lives.

Examples:	COD	NFL
	UPS	TMI
	RSVP	BFF
	IBM	ERP
	OSHA	NCLB
	FBI	MRP

However, if the readers are not familiar with the acronyms used, they may have trouble comprehending or following the meaning of the report. One helpful rule is to always spell out the words of the acronym *the first time it is used* in a report.

Examples:	Supply Chain Management (SCM)
	Enterprise Resource Planning (ERP)
	No Child Left Behind (NCLB)
	Material Resource Planning (MRP)
	Just-in-Time (JIT)

In addition, you can include a *List of Acronyms* on the page following the Contents. This inclusion allows the reader to easily look up the meaning of the acronyms.

Examples:	SCM	Supply Chain Management
	ERP	Enterprise Resource Planning
	NCLB	No Child Left Behind
	MRP	Material Resource Planning
	JIT	Just-in-Time

Capitalization

A common dilemma is deciding when to capitalize letters and when to use lowercase letters. This dilemma may be one of the reasons many people tend to use all capital letters—thus avoiding the decision entirely. All uppercase letters are hard to read and should be avoided.

These guidelines provide a foundation for determining what to capitalize. Capitalize the first letter of:

- The first word of a sentence
    Capitalize the first letter of the first word in a sentence.
- The first word of a direct quotation
    The leader said, "Go do your work."
- The first word following a colon
    Do yourself a favor: Practice your writing.
- The names of specific things, such as

– people	*Andi Gray*
– days and months	*Sunday, March*
– title of people	*Aunt Nettie*
(but not without the name—my aunt)	
– president and vice president of the United States	*the President*
– holidays	*Thanksgiving*
– geographic places	*France, Middle East*
– buildings and rooms	*Business Building*
– lakes and mountains	*Mono Lake*
– sections of the country	*the West*
(but not directions)	*west*
– nationalities and races	*German*
– languages	*English*
– ships and airplanes	*Santa Maria*
– space vehicles	*Discoverer*
– publications	*Newsweek*
– books and articles	*Report Writing—A Survival Guide*
(except for articles—a, an)	
(except for prepositions—of, to, in, on, for, etc.)	
(except for conjunctions—and, but, or, nor, etc.)	
– artistic works	*Mona Lisa*
– epithets	*the Big Apple*
– registered trademarks	*Xerox, Kleenex*

| – abbreviations | *MBA* |
| – acronyms | *BFF* |

Italics

Words and phrases are easier to read when italicized rather than underlined. Modern twenty-first century reports use italics to set words and phrases apart from the rest of the text.

Italics are useful to:

- Indicate names of books, magazines, newspapers, plays, and movies.
  - *Report Writing—A Survival Guide* will help you prepare effective reports.

- Mix foreign words with English words.
  - She said *"Buenos dias."*

- Place emphasis or highlight a word.
  - She was *guilty.*
  - Please *mark* the item that you want.

- Refer to a word as a word
  - The word *rush* was not used.

Numbers

Extreme accuracy is important when using numbers in reports. A writer must decide when to use a number as a figure and when to spell it out. A few basic rules to follow are listed.

- Numbers are spelled out for one through ten.
  The report surveys three companies.

- Figures are used for numbers larger than ten.
    The report surveys 50 companies.

- Numbers are spelled out when used as the first word of a sentence.
    Fifty years ago this company began operations.

- Figures are used:
    - in a listing when one of the numbers is higher than ten.
        The committee consists of 3 men and 17 women.

    - to express dates without *th* unless the number is before the month.
        February 20   20ᵗʰ of February

    - to express sums of money.
        $15 million or $15,000,000

    - to express chapter and page numbers.
        chapter 5, page 7

    - to express decimals, percentage, dimensions, weights, and temperatures.
        .15   15%   15 × 30   15 pounds   80°

- Omit the decimals in even-dollar figures, unless other numbers in the same sentence include cents.
        The cost of the report is $15.
        The costs of the reports are $15.00 and $21.50.

- Use words to represent time when o'clock is used but figures with p.m. or a.m.
        eight o'clock
        8 p.m. or 10 a.m.

- Omit the minutes unless another time is used in the same sentence where they are needed.
        8:30 p.m. or 10:00 a.m. or 9:00 to 5:30

- Use words for names of streets up to and including twelve.
  Third Avenue or First Street but 15th Street

Punctuation

Punctuation used correctly adds clarity to writing; used incorrectly it can confuse or even distort the meaning. The main types of punctuation are the apostrophe, colon, comma, dash, diagonal, ellipsis points, exclamation, hyphen, parentheses, period, question mark, quotation marks, semicolon, and underscore. A few general guidelines are reviewed for each of these types of punctuation.

Apostrophe

' The apostrophe shows possession. Use before the *s* if singular; use after if plural or if a word ends with *s*.
  – *Paul's report*
  – *boy's car but boys' car (if two boys own one car)*

' Indicates omissions in contractions and in dates.
  – *She can't read the report today.*
  – *The company was founded in '53.*

' Forms the plural of numbers, letters, and words.
  – *Mind your p's and q's.*
  – *The report was full of or's and nor's.*

Colon

: Use a colon before a list of items or a series of words—whether listed in the sentence or on separate lines.
  – *The following people are exempt: John, Robert, Edward, and Tom.*
  – *The following people are exempt:*

John	*Edward*
Robert	*Tom*

: Use a colon when the second clause explains or clarifies the first clause.
   – *Reports are vital in the world of business: without them, more meetings would be needed.*

Comma

, Use a comma to separate words, phrases, and clauses in a series.
   – *Report preparation consists of planning, writing, and editing.*

, Use a comma between two adjectives.
   – *The attractive, efficient report . . .*

, Use a comma to separate two main clauses.
   – *The report is difficult, and the research will require several days.*

, Use a comma to set off introductory phrases.
   – *Frequently, the work requires . . .*

, Use a comma to set off words, phrases, or clauses that interrupt a sentence.
   – *The work, being completed by a committee, is . . .*
   – *She is, in my opinion, a . . .*
   – *The boss, Robert Smith, is . . .*

Dash

— Use a dash to show an afterthought or a summation.
   – *Refer to a piece of art before it appears—not after.*
   – *The staff—including clerical workers, managers, and executives— is to . . .*

— Use a dash to indicate a sudden change of thought.
   – *The report was due last week—but remember the workers were sent home when the water pipes broke.*

Report Writing—A Survival Guide

Diagonal

/   Use a diagonal or slash or one of the two or both in the expression *and/or*.
- *Susan and/or Mark will write the report.*

/   Use a diagonal or slash in fractions, with abbreviations, or with discount terms.
- *6 2/3   c/o   2/10   n/30*

Ellipsis

...   Use an ellipsis to indicate the omission of parts of a quotation. If at the end of a sentence, use four dots—the period at the end of the sentence accounts for the fourth dot.
- *"The people will arrive . . . after the event."*
- *"The people will arrive . . . . "*

Exclamation Point

!   Use an exclamation point to indicate excitement, emotion, or a command.
- *The end is near!*

Hyphen

-    Use a hyphen in compound surnames.
  - Rhodes-Rivera

-    Use a hyphen to separate numbers such as in telephone or social security numbers.
  - *(909) 869-1000 or 512-34-0000*

-    Use a hyphen when two adjectives work together to modify a noun.
  - *well-written book* or *first-rate hotel*

- Use a hyphen in word division at the end of a line when lines fall short or are too long. *(See Word Division rules.)*
  - *profes- sor*   or   *knowl- edge*

Parentheses

( ) Use parentheses to set off nonessential explanatory words, phrases, or sentences—the use is stronger than a comma but not as strong as a dash.
  - *Please show your costs (lines 73-25).*

Period

. Use a period at the end of a sentence.
  - *The meeting ended.*

. Use a period in abbreviations and decimals.
  - *Dr.   Blvd.   5.8%*
. Use a period to separate numbers in telephone numbers.
  - *512.34.5489*

Question Mark

? Use a question mark at the end of any sentence asking a question with an answer expected.
  - *When is the report due?*

? Use a question mark in parentheses to express doubt.
  - *The company was founded in 1980(?).*

Quotation Marks

" " Use quotation marks to enclose a direct quotation. Periods and commas go inside the quotation marks; colons, dashes, and semicolons go outside the quotations marks. Exclamation points and question marks go inside the quotation marks if they are part of the quoted material and outside if they are not.

- *She said, "The air is bad."*
- *Did she say "The air is bad"?*

" " Use quotation marks to enclose titles, words, or phrases borrowed from others or used in a special way.
- *The "Supply Chain Lab" is now open.*
- *A "magic" atmosphere was created.*

Semicolon

; Use a semicolon to join two independent clauses not separated by a coordinating conjunction such as *and, but, or, nor,* etc.
- *The work is completed; the report will be mailed next week.*

; Use a semicolon to connect two main clauses using a conjunctive adverb such as *however, nevertheless, consequently, therefore, moreover, hence,* and *furthermore.*
- *The work is not completed; however, it will be mailed by the end of the month.*

; Use a semicolon to clarify series of words and phrases requiring other internal comma punctuation.
- *The executive staff consists of John Johnston, President; Marcia West, Vice-President; Susan Miller, Secretary; and Ron Smith, Treasurer.*

Spelling

Correct spelling is imperative in any written report if you want to create a favorable image. Spellchecks are available on software programs; however, the spellchecks are unable to pick up some types of errors.

The following list of words illustrates types of errors that would not be found by a spellchecker on the computer. You can use a regular dictionary or the dictionary in your software to be sure you have the right word.

accede	exceed
accept	except
access	excess
ad	add
adapt	adept
addition	edition
advice	advise
affect	effect
all ready	already
all ways	always
allowed	aloud
any way	anyway
are	our, hour
capital	capitol
cease	seize
cite	sight, site
complement	compliment
council	counsel
descent	dissent
desert	dessert
device	devise
disapprove	disprove
disburse	disperse
dual	duel
elicit	illicit
emigrate	immigrate
expand	expend
farther	further
foreword	forward
formally	formerly
forth	fourth
incidence	incidents
interstate	intrastate
its	it's
knew	new

Report Writing—A Survival Guide

later	latter
leased	least
lessen	lesson
maybe	may be
passed	past
personal	personnel
principal	principle
role	roll
stationary	stationery
suit	suite
than	then
their	there
to	too, two
weak	week
weather	whether

Word Division

Dividing words at the end of a line can be another difficult decision. Many word processing and production programs include a feature that will allow you to control the word divisions used within your report.

You may choose to manually control hyphenation (referred to as force hyphenate). Some of the programs will give you suggestions on acceptable word divisions. However, you will need to be aware of a few general guidelines in making wise decisions on when, where, and how to divide.

A good rule of word division is *don't*! However, you may find that you must sometimes divide words to make lines end evenly on the right or, if using full justification, to prevent large spaces between words. You may even find, on occasion, that to have proper line endings you need to rewrite, rearrange, or restate your thought. If you must divide words, use the following guidelines.

Guidelines for *Not* Dividing Words

The first and last lines of a paragraph or a page.
More than two lines in a row.
Five or fewer letters such as *cable, icon, and idea.*
Only two letters should appear on the next line such as in ~~careful-ly~~ instead of *care-fully.*
Only one letter left on a line so no division.

Guidelines *for* Dividing Words

Only between syllables—thus, one-syllable words cannot be divided.
Keep a single-vowel syllable with the first part of the word such as ~~form-ulation~~ instead of formu-lation.
Divide compound words between the two words such as in *sales-person* and desk-top.

Chapter 6

Producing

> **Producing includes the techniques needed to make your reports appealing to your readers. The design elements of fonts, color, paper, layout, and graphics will provide you with ideas that will make your report stand out.**
>
> **—Kupsh and Rhodes**

Today's technology makes it possible for you to create high-quality reports. No longer do your reports have to look like diaries or essays. Instead, they can look like professional publications.

Fonts

In working with fonts, you need to consider the classifications, kinds, size, spacing, alignment, and a variety of other characteristics. The choices you make can greatly affect the impression your report projects—be sure that the impression is favorable and conveys the appropriate and desired message.

Classifications

The default font is frequently set at Times New Roman, which ends up being the one used by most people. Many other fonts are more appropriate and easier to read. In addition, different font styles can serve different purposes. This book uses Calibri for the body and Franklin Gothic for the headings and subheadings.

Hundreds of fonts are available. Having the appropriate, distinctive font can make your report stand out. The classifications of fonts fall into four areas—professional, formal, casual, and headings and subheadings. The following lists consist of categories of fonts selected by the authors.

Headings/Subheadings Professional Fonts. These fonts (shown in size 12) are appropriate for most reports. Research reports, case studies, feasibility studies, strategic plans, business plans, and business proposals are reports that would lend themselves to business professional fonts. Fonts may vary according to your software.

Professional Fonts
Arial
Arial Narrow
Arial Rounded MT Bold
Adobe Garamond Pro
Adobe Caslon Pro
Calibri
Garamond
Kozuka Gothic Pro M
Tahoma
Tekton Pro
Verdana

Headings/Subheadings Fonts. These fonts (shown in size 14) can be mixed with the professional fonts. The business professional fonts would be used for the body of the report.

Heading/Subheadings Fonts

Arial Rounded MT

Bodoni MT Black

Cooper Black

Elephant

Franklin Gothic Heavy

Formal Fonts. Formal fonts are appropriate for e-mail signatures, brochures, newsletters, and invitations. Be sure these fonts are large enough to be read easily.

Formal Fonts

Baskerville Old Face

Brush Scripte Std

Edwardian Sc4ript TFC

Forte

French Script

Harlow Solid Italic

Lucida Handwriting

Casual Fonts. Casual fonts are appropriate for e-mail signatures, brochures, newsletters, and invitations. Be sure these fonts are large enough to be easily read.

Casual Fonts

Chiller

Comic Sans MS

Hobo Std

Jokerman

Poplar Std

Snap ITC

Variations

A variety of decisions are needed when working with fonts. With good choices, these variations can make your report have that extra "zing." A font usually means a complete set of characters *(the full alphabet, numbers, and symbols)* in one thickness and style. Fonts come in all the variations of a basic design in every thickness and size.

Plain, Bold, Italics, etc. These variations include bold, italics or oblique, bold italics, shadow, outline, and strikethrough. If used correctly, these features add not only to the attractiveness of a report but increase the readability.

Plain	
Bold	~~Strikethrough~~
Italics	<u>Underscore</u>
Bold Italics	

Condensed, Narrow, and Expanded. Many fonts are also available in condensed, narrow, or expanded versions. These variations are particularly helpful when the writer wants to say a lot in a small space or expand a few words to fill a larger space.

Thickness. The thickness of the strokes making up the letters is another choice affecting the size or look of a letter. Terms used to distinguish among the thickness of a font in a specific size are extra light, light, regular, medium, semi bold, bold, extra bold, heavy, or ultra bold.

Uppercase and Lowercase. Printed materials using lowercase and uppercase are more distinctive and easier to read.

ALL CAPS ARE HARD TO READ.
Lowercase is easier to read.

Therefore, putting words, phrases, lines, or paragraphs in all uppercase letters tends to make the words harder to read rather than easier to read.

Underscoring. Underscoring should be reserved for Web links and e-mails. If you have the urge to underscore, avoid doing so, but draw a line underneath the word(s) or put a box around the word(s).

Reverse Type. Headings in reverse type—white or light characters on a dark background—offer an eye-catching combination for headings. However, too much reverse type can become difficult to read.

Reverse

Drop Caps. Another variation possible for the beginning of a chapter or a new section is the use of a drop cap. Note the drop caps in the example below as well as those used in this book.

A drop cap is a good beginning
for a chapter or section.

Sizes

Text can range from 2 points to extremely large sizes (see examples on the right). The logical size for text body ranges from 10 points to 12 points, depending on a particular font. Headings are normally made

7 9 10 11 12 14 18
20 24 36

in bold and or italics to capture the reader's attention and can vary in size to show the level of importance. In general, the larger the letters, the more important the heading!

Line Spacing

Line spacing can be varied for a more pleasing look. Copy may be 12-point font size with 14 points of line spacing or, as the illustration shows, 10 points with 15 points for line spacing.

This is an example of 10-point font using 15-point line spacing.

Alignment

Font alignment (left, right, centered, or justified) is possible either before or after the words are keyed into the computer. Justification, making both the left and right margins flush, gives a report a blocked look and is preferred by some

Left

    Centered

        Right

individuals. However, justification should not be used if it causes large blank spaces to run through the copy as shown by the arrows.

However, justification should not be used if doing so causes blank spaces to run through the copy.

This second box shows an example of justification without extra-large blank spaces between the words.

Hyphenating words, either through the software or by manually forcing words to be divided, can help to prevent large blank spaces and give the copy a tighter look. Hyphenation rules should be followed.

Uneven line endings provide a visual crutch for the eyes in addition to giving a more artistic look to the page. While research has shown that readability is improved if a ragged right margin is used, the report with a right justified margin looks very professional. The choice is one for personal judgment.

Color

Color can be used for paper, covers, and fonts. Reports do not have to be an all black and white affair. Many reports and books are still printed with black ink on white paper. However, font colors can add to the attraction of your report. Be sure that the font color used is dark enough to provide a good contrast with the paper.

If photos are included in the report, a very white paper will show the light highlights better and make the dark inks seem darker. On the other hand, you may want to use paper that is slightly off-white (natural, cream, ivory, eggshell, mellow, or soft white) to reduce the glare in very technical manuals that require readers to spend a considerable amount of reading time. Also, the use of a light color can make your report stand out from others in the stack, which is especially important if you are submitting a proposal where there is competition for a bid. Color is also useful in coding material.

Advantages of Using Color
Quick identification of sections.
Glossaries or appendices to allow for easy referencing.
Section or chapter heading of each new section.
Covers and a neutral white, off-white, or beige for the inside.
Fonts as long as they are dark enough to provide a contrast.

Paper

Paper comes in different types, weights, and sizes. The quality of the paper reflects the professionalism of the report.

Type

Paper types include bond, matte, or glossy. A glossy paper provides a more sophisticated look and is better for halftones and color printing. Even without halftones, however, printing on glossy paper will be clearer.

Some types of paper have a right side and a wrong side. Therefore, if only one side of the paper is to be used, printing should be on the right side. When you place the ream so that you can read the label, the right side of the paper will be on top.

Papers with a high rag or cotton content are more expensive but age better with less deterioration in color and context. Papers made without any rag content are more economical and good only for reports that will be read and sent to the recycling bin within a short time.

Weight

When paper is cut, the result is four stacks of 8 ½ x 11 sheets. Thus, the weight of four reams of paper represents the weight on the package. A twenty-four-pound weight is a good choice for most reports. If you are printing on both sides of the paper, you need to get a heavier weight and determine that the front side of the sheet does not bleed through to the back.

Size

Most writers assume that they will print their report on standard 8 ½ × 11 inch paper. However, many possibilities are available. Even if your printer accepts only standard or legal-size paper, you are not held to these sizes because the paper can be trimmed to a desired size after printing.

Layout

Many considerations and decisions are required in creating a vision of the final document. These considerations are page orientation, margins, column size, blank space, headings and subheadings, page numbers, headers and footers, and binding and covers.

Page Orientation

Page orientation is either portrait (vertical) or landscape (horizontal) and should be decided at the start. People tend to use portrait because they are used to it; however, a landscape orientation might work very effectively. Not all pages of the report have to be one way. Using landscape orientation is very effective for displaying large spreadsheets or large pictures within a report. Landscaped pages are displayed effectively when the top of the page is the binding side of the report.

Margins

Adequate margins should be left to give each and every page a frame or border. Top and bottom as well as the left and right margins should all be even unless the document is to be bound. *The amount of room left for the binding will vary according to the type of binding used—see later topic on Binding.* However, you must determine the type of binding desired before determining your margin settings. On a standard page of 8 ½ x 11, you will normally need to allow a quarter of an inch to a half inch of extra space for the binding.

Column Size

Research has shown that it is possible to read faster and comprehend more information when shorter lines are used. The actual length of the line will, of course, depend upon the page size. If you are using standard size (8 ½ × 11), you may want to consider using a columnar layout format. A columnar format works great for a business report. You want the reader(s) to find it easy and pleasurable to read—not dull and boring.

Blank Space

Blank space is very important for a professional look. Actually, each page should contain approximately 50 percent or more blank space. Pages with too much type and art give the appearance of being too heavy and hard to read.

Headings and Subheadings

Headings and subheadings are crucial in helping the busy readers of today. Effective writing requires headings and subheadings to help the readers keep focused. Remember that a reader may be interrupted with a phone call, visitor, or some other distraction—causing the mind to wander. Headings and subheadings can do wonders in helping to keep readers focused as well as allow readers to scan the copy for parts that are of particular interest to them. Headings and subheadings can be considered as the elements that make up an outline.

Guidelines for Headings and Subheadings
Make headings and subheadings concise but descriptive—possibly attention getting.
Follow parallel construction—verb and noun or nouns only.
Break the divisions down so that a heading or subheading always has two or more listings.
Make the headings and subheadings agree with the contents, although the contents may omit minor subheads and list only two or three levels.

A hierarchy of sizes and styles is needed for showing the various levels of headings or subheadings. The hierarchy style should be consistent and logical and progress from higher to lower levels in an obvious pattern. For instance, check the examples in the box. The hierarchy style can be identified and stored in your word processing software.

First-level Subhead 18 Bold
Second-level Subhead 14 Bold
Third-level Subhead 12 Bold Italics
Fourth-level Subhead Bold Italics Indented

Page Numbers

Any time you have more than one or two pages, you need to number them. Software has the capability of performing this function automatically, but you must determine where you want the page numbers. Several choices are acceptable—either the upper or lower outside corners or the middle of the bottom of the page. Placing the numbers on the outside corners allows readers to locate a specific page more easily when scanning through a report.

Page numbers should start with the second page of the body of the report. This page is numbered 2. The Title Page, Contents, and other preliminary pages are typically not numbered. You may find it necessary to put these pages in a separate document so the software doesn't automatically insert page numbers. More formal documents such as theses and dissertations use Arabic numbers (i, ii, iii, iv, v, etc.) for the preliminary pages.

Headers and Footers

In today's busy world, readers frequently scan written material rapidly rather than reading it thoroughly from front to back. These readers are helped in locating or identifying a particular section or area of a report if headers (identifying information at the top of a page) and footers (identifying information at the bottom of a page) are used. Headers and footers should not be confused with footnotes. Variations are possible, but one logical system is to have the left-facing page show the overall title and the right-facing page show the chapter or section title. Thus, a reader can quickly check the name of the document and also focus in on the specific subject.

Binding

Binding is that added step that can make a good first impression, as well as keep the report organized. Remember, the binding determines the amount of your left margin. The binding of your report depends upon how many pages and the type of impression you want to make. Small reports of 20 of fewer pages can be stapled. Holes can be punched in order to place your report in a three-ring binder. Many other options are available with wire or spiral binding being good choices. Be careful that you do not select a binding that will fall apart easily.

Cover

A customized cover on a report can set it apart from others. The cover of a report can vary from ordinary title pages, to front and back pages using heavier paper, to specially ordered personalized notebooks.

Studies by General Binding Corporation show that a report is twice as likely to be read and three times as likely to be saved if it is attractively bound.

Graphics

Anything on a page other than text is referred to as graphics. When used in a document, graphics should clarify, add to, illustrate, or enhance the document in some way. Line after line of text is boring and readers tend to skip over information. Graphics can improve the readability of the report. However, graphics should not be used without a specific reason or purpose. Otherwise, the inclusion of graphics may be distracting and confusing rather than helpful to your readers.

Illustrations should be labeled and referred to in the text. More formal documents may refer to any of the graphic illustrations as Figure 1 or Illustration 1 (followed with the title). The label can be above or below and left justified

Figure 1—Yearly Sales

or centered. The labeling makes it easier for readers with the text saying "as shown in Figure 1 . . ."

Lines, Boxes, Shapes, Background Tints, Patterns and Borders. Lines, boxes, shapes, background tints, and patterns are helpful in making documents more stimulating and appealing to readers.

Lines, boxes, and shading are useful in creating divisions or focusing attention upon a given area. Icons or symbols available in various fonts may 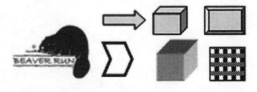 help focus or direct the reader's attention. Logos provide a subtle way of marketing your company or providing a theme for a product or topic. Additional graphics can include page borders and a watermark used as a background.

Photos and Clip Art. Photographs or clip art are available online. Or you can add your own original  photographs or drawings. For instance if you want a picture of a building, you can use clip art to portray the image. But if a real photo is available, you can project a more realistic image for the reader. Be sure to cite the source of the graphic or picture if it is not yours.

Tables. Using a table to list items is a variation of bullet lists. For instance, if you want to show the various kinds of graphics, you could use a table similar to the one at the end of this chapter. This one has one column and five rows, but you could have numerous columns as well as any number of rows.

Types of Graphics
Lines, boxes, shapes, background tints, patterns, and borders
Photos and clipart
Tables
Charts and graphs

Charts and Graphs. Information containing and comparing numbers is easier to visualize in a chart or graph than when expressed in words only. Spreadsheets developed in Microsoft Excel, Word, and PowerPoint make information easy to display. The chart/graph below displays information on what employers want from grads according to an article in *USA Today*, Thursday, January 21, 2010. The information was from a survey by Peter D. Hart Research Associates which was based on interviews with 302 employers who have at least 25 employees and who report that 25 percent of new hires hold either a two-year or four-year college degree.

What Employers Want

Connect Choices & Actions to Ethical Decisions	75%
Analytic Skill & Complex Problem Solving	75%
Apply Knowledge & Skills To Real World Settings	79%
Critical Thinking & Analytic Reasoning Skills	81%
Effective Oral & Written Communications Skills	89%

Source: *USA Today*, Thursday, January 21, 2010, p. 7D

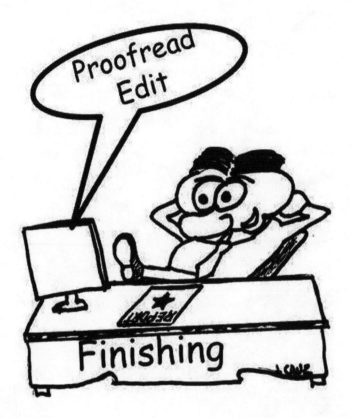

Chapter 7

Finishing

Think you are finished? Think again! All your hard work can be wasted if you do not follow through with the finishing touches of your report.

—Rhodes and Kupsh

If readers see errors in the first few pages, your credibility may be lost and the report is not read. An important aspect of a report is accuracy and meticulousness. Little errors can make a big difference—the unfavorable kind. Therefore, the final step in finishing a report is to edit and proofread your report carefully.

Ask other people to edit and proofread the report for you. You might want to assign them different tasks—similar to those performed by the staff in publishing a book. Editing and proofreading are needed to make sure that your report is accurate as well as meticulous in its final form.

Editing

Three different types of editing are required for any report—substance, style, and consistency. Even though these can be completed by you or another person, it may be better to think of these as separate activities. Trying to do everything at once is hard; most people have trouble completing three things at the same time.

Substance

Before giving the report a more detailed scrutiny, a general content look is needed. Questions under consideration during this editing process are as follows:

Editing Questions
Is the material complete?
Should any of the content be omitted?
Is the information correct?
Is the content presented in the right order?
Is any reorganization needed?
Are there better ways of presenting some of the information, such as graphs, tables, artwork, etc.?
Does any rewriting need to be done?
Is your report eye-catching and easy to read?

Style

Several types of style should be considered during the editing. First, is the writing consistent with the recommended styles described in Chapter 4 **Writing** and the style manuals for referencing discussed in Chapter 2 **Starting**? Next, have the styles or rules of your particular organization been followed properly? Some companies have their own corporate style guides. Teachers may also request a particular style.

Consistency

Another type of editing involves looking for consistency. Details in style should be consistent; possibly several ways are correct, but one way should be chosen and used throughout the report. If you are working with a team, proofing for consistency is really necessary. Other types of consistency are listed under the next section on proofreading.

Proofreading

Proofreading your own work is hard and not very efficient. Because you are so familiar with the report, you tend to race through and think of the bigger picture, the next report, the slides you need to make when you present the report, or whatever. Someone else who has not been working on the report can give it a much fresher and more efficient look.

Techniques

If no one is available and you are forced to be the one and only one to proofread your own work, you may want to use some special proofing techniques. These techniques would also be good for your proofreaders to follow.

Proofreading Techniques
Use a ruler to slow down your reading and make yourself read line by line.
Read the report out loud. This process slows down your reading and makes you listen to how it really sounds.
Read each line backward. The work will not make sense, but typographical errors will stand out.
Limit your proofreading to small bits at any one time. You could take frequent breaks or limit yourself to a section or chapter a day. Try to do your final check the day after you finish writing.
Proofread when you are most fresh. This time may be early morning or whatever time of the day is your peak for best performance.

Try to proofread when you know you will have peace and quiet and can avoid interruptions from the telephone or visitors.
Print a copy for proofreading. On-screen proofreading is far more difficult.

Tips

Proofreading is a very important step—not to be neglected. Your computer may not catch all errors. During proofreading, you and your other proofreaders may find the following list helpful in looking for errors.

Proofreading Tips
Does the report make sense?
Are there any typographical errors?
Are words divided correctly throughout the document?
If right justification is used, should any words be force hyphenated to avoid large blank spaces between words?
Are words on the first and last lines of a page or paragraph divided?
Do you always have at least two lines in a paragraph on a page?
Do you have no more than 10-12 lines per paragraph?
Is the style consistent throughout—fonts, spacing, indenting, headings, etc.?
Is capitalization correct and consistent?
Is spelling correct and consistent?
Are numbers either given as figures or written out correctly and consistently?
Do quotation marks and parentheses always have both a beginning and an ending?
Do verbs and subjects agree?
Is the correct word used in words that sound alike—*their* and *there*; *two, to,* and *too*; *sense* and *cents, its* and *it's*, etc.?

Report Writing—A Survival Guide

CONTINUED
Are complete sentences used, and do they make sense?
Are all numbers accurate?
Are all totals correctly added?

Checklists

Use the checklists as a tool in the following instances:

- Before you write your report
- While you are writing your report
- After the first draft of your report
- When your report is finished

For each question, answer one of the following:

_____ Yes
_____ No

If your answer is **No** or you are not sure, review the appropriate section and confirm that your report is correct, or change the incorrect parts.

Chapter 1—Organizing

If your answer is **No** or you are not sure, check the contents or the index for the page number to find the information regarding that topic.

Purpose	Yes	No
Have you determined the purpose of your report? Inform Interpret Recommend Persuade		

Type	Yes	No
Have you determined the type of report you are going to write? Research Report Case Study Analysis Case Study Feasibility Study Strategic Plan Business Plan Business Proposal Evaluation Report Synthesis Report Assessment/Audit Report Technical Report Follow-up Report Press Release Miscellaneous		

Format Style	Yes	No

Have you determined what format style is appropriate?
    E-mail, Memo, Letter
    Form
    Report
    Newsletter
    Brochure
    Magazine, Booklet, or Manual
    Social Media		

Parts	Yes	No

Do you have all the necessary parts?
    Executive Summary/Abstract
    Title Page
    Contents
    Introduction
    Body
    Bibliography/References/Resources
    Appendices		

Chapter 2—Starting

If your answer is **No** or you are not sure, check the contents or the index for the page number to find the information regarding that topic.

Planning	Yes	No
Did you have a detailed scheme or method worked out beforehand for the accomplishment of an objective?		
Did you establish an organized overall plan?		
Are the purposes and objectives of your report clearly stated?		
Did you set up a time schedule for each of the sections?		
Is your report written for the target audience? • What is the educational level of the intended audience? • How much background or technical experience do members of your intended audience have on the topic? • Will the audience be expecting a formal or informal report? • What type of action—a verbal response, a written reaction, or an interview—do you anticipate from the audience? • Are you addressing the appropriate audience?		
Researching	**Yes**	**No**
Did you collect the data?		
Did you include enough relevant existing sources?		
Did you include the relevant original sources?		

Outlining	Yes	No
Do you have a complete, organized list of what is to be covered in the report?		
Do you have a parallel hierarchy of topics and subtopics?		
Are the topics and subtopics descriptive and functional rather than attention-getting ones?		
Are there two or more points within each subtopic?		
Do you have a logical or sequential arrangement of topics and subtopics?		

Report Writing—A Survival Guide

Chapter 3—Referencing

If your answer is **No** or you are not sure, check the contents or the index for the page number to find the information regarding that topic.

References	Yes	No
Did you use a reference management software?		
Did you block or indent direct quotations of 5 lines or more than 40 words by indenting from both margins by approximately 5 spaces or half an inch?		
Did you insert your comments between brackets in the quotations?		
Did you indicate omissions from the original quote by using ellipsis points—a series of three periods (. . .)?		
Did you include a quotation of less than 5 lines or 40 words in the text using quotation marks to distinguish it from your writing?		
Did you select only the most relevant portion if a direct quotation is more than a page or so in length or simply refer to it in the text of the report and include it as an appendix?		
Did you mention in the report at the appropriate place items in the appendix?		
Did you paraphrase or summarize (restating material in your own words) as an indirect quotation?		
Even though quotation marks are not used, could a reader tell exactly what is paraphrased and what is your own work by using the following: to Xxx, . . . ; Xxx states that . . .; Xxx found that . . . ?		

Sources	Yes	No
Did you use either (1) parenthetical references, (2) footnotes, or (3) endnotes?		
In parenthetical references, did you place a shortened reference within the text?		
Did you include a complete listing of these sources at the end of the section, chapter, or report?		
Did you place the last name of the author and the date in parentheses separated by a comma for parenthetical references? The name of a corporation, the name of a work, or some other means of identification may also be used with the date.		
If the author's name is mentioned in the text, did you use only the date in parentheses? If you refer to both the author and the date in the text, nothing needs to be put in parentheses.		
Did you include the reference in the alphabetical listing at the end?		
If the quote is from a specific page, did you include the page number in case a reader wants to locate the original writing?		
Did you indicate endnotes in the text by a raised number, or a number in parenthesis on the same line as the text?		
Did you delete any footnotes at the bottom of the page if you used endnotes?		
Did you include a complete listing of the sources in numerical order at the end of the report along with an alphabetized list of those same references?		
Did you use footnotes correctly by placing a raised number in the text at the end of the quotation—either direct or paraphrased and then placing the identification at the bottom of the page under a one-inch line?		
Did you use a complete listing of the reference the first time it appears?		
Did you use a shortened version of the subsequent references to the same work?		

CONTINUED		
Did you omit the use of Latin abbreviations—*ibid, op. cit,* and *loc. cit.?* They tend to be confusing and are no longer used.		
Did you make sure that the footnote appears on the page where it was used and that proper spacing is left at the bottom of the page?		
Do you have a complete listing of sources at the end of the section, chapter, or report?		

Using Style Manuals	Yes	No
Did you use one of the popular style guides or manuals?		
Did you try to establish some logical arrangement and use common sense in unique items?		

Avoiding Plagiarism	Yes	No
Did you cite the reference when you paraphrased or summarized words or ideas?		
Did you use quotation marks and cite the reference when you used the exact words of someone?		
Did you reference or give credit if you used a paper from a previous class?		

Chapter 4—Writing

If your answer is **No** or you are not sure, check the contents or the index for the page number to find the information regarding that topic.

Objectivity	Yes	No
Did you write your report from an objective standpoint?		
Did you eliminate any personal emotions and opinions?		
Does your report include facts and findings?		
Do your facts and findings lead to recommendations and conclusions formed on the basis of those facts and findings?		
Did you look at all sides of the problem with an open mind before stating your conclusions?		
Did you take on the role of a referee at a sporting event or a judge presiding in court?		
Are your decisions based on the results, the evidence, or an interpretation of the results and evidence?		
Did you use proper nouns and the occasional use of *he, him, she, her, they,* and *them?*		

Conciseness	Yes	No
Did you eliminate information that is irrelevant to the report?		
Did you eliminate redundancy—useless repetition of words?		
Did you combine clutter and clichés in a way that does not waste words?		
Did you use compound adjectives to reduce the number of words?		
Did you substitute a precise word or words for phrases?		
Did you avoid restating implied (obvious) ideas?		
Did you cite specific examples for each abstract word?		

Coherence	Yes	No
Is your writing coherent by linking the thought from one sentence to the next and from one paragraph to the next?		
Did you link by repeating words and by using a transition?		
Did you repeat a word either directly or with a similar word?		
Did you use transitional words—such as *an explanation, enumeration or listing, similarity or contrast, and cause or effect, as well as, for example, for instance, to illustrate.*		
Did you use bullet lists with numbers or symbols when appropriate?		
Did you use transition words to show a similarity or a contrast between two situations?		
Did you use transitional words—such as *because of, therefore, thus, as a result, for this reason, consequently*—to show a cause or an effect?		

Tone	Yes	No
Did you accentuate the positive and eliminate the negative?		
Did you write in active voice—with the subject doing the acting?		
Did you avoid expletives—such as *there are, it is, it is noted that, it is understood that, etc.?*		
Did you use a noun or the pronouns *he, she, him, her, they,* and *them (avoiding* I, my, we, our)?		
Did you eliminate any tone in your writing that reflects a gender bias or any other type of bias—*race, religion, age, disability, or ethnic group?*		
Did you avoid stereotyping by changing to plural form when possible or referring to both genders?		
Did you eliminate the use of biased titles and substitute a more neutral word?		

Emphasis	Yes	No
Did you decide on your most important word or phrase and then decide whether you want that word or phrase to make an initial or a lasting impact?		

Variety & Comprehensive	Yes	No
Did you vary the length of sentences and paragraphs and mix simple sentences with complex or compound sentences?		
Does your report include all the necessary parts?		

Chapter 5—Polishing

If your answer is **No** or you are not sure, check the contents or the index for the page number to find the information regarding that topic.

Abbreviations	Yes	No
Did you use abbreviations correctly and appropriately?		

Acronyms	Yes	No
Did you use acronyms that your audience knows?		
Did you spell out the acronym the first time it was used?		
Did you include a list of acronyms after the table of contents?		

Capitalization	Yes	No
Did you capitalize the: • first word of a sentence, • first word of a direct quotation, • first word following a colon, • names of specific things?		

Italics	Yes	No
Did you use italics to: • indicate names of books, magazines, newspapers, plays, and movies, • mix foreign words with English words, • place emphasis or highlight a word, • refer to a word as a word?		

Numbers	Yes	No
Did you use the following rules for numbers? • Spell out numbers for one through ten. • Use figures for numbers larger than ten. • Spell out numbers if the first word of a sentence. • Use figures in a listing when one of the numbers is higher than ten. • Use figures to express dates without *th* unless the number is before the month. • Use figures to express sums of money. • Use figures to express chapter and page numbers. • Use figures to express decimals, percentage, dimensions, weights, and temperatures. • Omit the zeroes and decimals unless other numbers in the same sentence include cents. • Use words to represent time when *o'clock* is used but figures with *p.m.* or *a.m.* • Omit the minutes unless another time is used in the same sentence where they are needed. • Use words for names of streets up to and including twelve.		

Punctuation	Yes	No
Did you use punctuation (apostrophe, colon, comma, dash, diagonal, ellipsis points, exclamation, hyphen, parentheses, period, question mark, quotation marks, semicolon, and underscore) correctly?		

Spelling	Yes	No
Did you use the spellcheck?		
Did you evaluate your report for errors that may not be found by the spellcheck?		
Did you have someone else check for errors?		

Report Writing—A Survival Guide

Word Division	Yes	No
Did you avoid the division of words: • in the first and last lines of a paragraph or page, • in more than two lines in a row, • if only one letter is left on the first line, • if only five or fewer letters?		
Did you divide: • only between syllables, • compound words between the two words, • words containing a hyphen at the hyphen?		
Did you keep a single-vowel syllable with the first part of the word?		

Chapter 6—Producing

If your answer is **No** or you are not sure, check the contents or the index for the page number to find the information regarding that topic.

Fonts	Yes	No
Did you choose an appropriate font(s) from the four classifications for your report?		
Did you take advantage or use any of the variations below: • plain, bold, italics, • condensed, narrow, expanded, • thickness, • uppercase, lowercase, • underscoring, • reverse type, • drop caps?		
Did you avoid underlining except for Web sites and e-mail addresses?		
Is the font for the body of your report between 8 and 12 points?		
Did you use appropriate line spacing?		
Did you make appropriate use of right/center/left alignment?		
If you justified the margins, did you avoid large blank spaces?		
Color	Yes	No
Did you take advantage of color (if appropriate) as follows? • Quick identification of sections. • Glossaries or appendices to allow for easy referencing. • Section or chapter heading of each new section. • Colored covers and a neutral white, off-white, or beige for the inside. • Fonts as long as they are easy to read.		

Paper	Yes	No
Did you select an appropriate weight of paper?		

Layout	Yes	No
Did you determine whether a landscape or portrait layout was more appropriate?		
Were margins reasonable?		
Did you leave room for the binding?		
Is the column size reasonable?		
Is there sufficient blank space on each page?		
Did you make headings and subheadings concise but descriptive?		
Do you have parallel construction using all verbs or all nouns in the listings?		
Did you break the divisions down so that a heading or subheading always has two or more listings?		
Did you make the headings and subheadings agree with the contents?		
Are your pages numbered correctly?		
Did you make use of headers and footers?		
Is your report attractively bound?		
Did you use an attractive cover?		

Graphics	Yes	No
Does your report include graphics as needed to help the readers?		
Did you include lines, boxes, shapes, background tints, and patterns?		
Did you include clip art and photos as appropriate?		
Did you use tables to list items in addition to bullet lists?		
When using numbers, did you display them as charts or graphs?		

Chapter 7—Finishing

If your answer is **No** or you are not sure, check the index for the page number to find the information regarding that topic.

Edit	Yes	No
Is the material complete?		
Should any of the content be omitted?		
Is the information correct?		
Is the content presented in the right order?		
Is any reorganization needed?		
Are there better ways of presenting some of the information, such as graphs, tables, artwork, etc.?		
Does any rewriting need to be done?		
Did you follow the style from one of the style manuals?		
Did you follow the style or rules for your particular company or a style requested by your teacher?		
Are you consistent in details of your style?		
Proofread	**Yes**	**No**
Have you read using a ruler to slow down your reading and make yourself read line by line?		
Did you read the report out loud?		
Did you read each line backward?		
Did you limit your proofreading to small bits at any one time?		
Did you proofread when you are most fresh?		
Did you try to proofread when you know you will have peace and quiet and can avoid interruptions from the telephone or visitors?		

Continued	Yes	No
Does the report make sense?		
Are there any typographical errors?		
Are words divided correctly throughout the document?		
If right justification is used, should any words be force hyphenated to avoid large blank spaces between words?		
Did you avoid having words on the first and last lines of a page or paragraph divided?		
Do you always have at least two lines in a paragraph on a page?		
Is the style consistent throughout—fonts, spacing, indenting, headings, etc.?		
Is capitalization correct and consistent?		
Is spelling correct and consistent?		
Are numbers either given as figures or written out correctly and consistently?		
Do quotation marks and parentheses always have both a beginning and an ending?		
Do verbs and subjects agree?		
Is the correct word used in words that sound alike—*their* and *there*; *two, to,* and *too*; *sense* and *cents*, *its* and *it's*, etc.?		
Are complete sentences used and do they make sense?		
Are all numbers accurate?		
Are all totals correctly added?		

INDEX

A

abbreviations 74, 82, 123
abstract 31
abstract or general words 63
acronyms 74-75, 123
active vs passive 67
alignment 94
APA reference list 53
apostrophe 79
appendices 34
appendix 34
assessment report 24
audit report 24
avoiding plagiarism 54

B

bias-free language 68
bibliographies 34
binding 100
blank space 98
body 33
booklet 28
brochure 27
business plan 23
business proposal 23

C

capitalization 75
case study 21
case study analysis 20
charts and graphs 102
checklists 106-126
citation creators 51
citing sources 51
    endnotes 52, 118
    footnotes 52, 118
    parenthetical 51, 118
clutter and clichés 62

coherence 64
colon 79-80, 82
color 95
column size 97
comma 52, 65, 80, 82-83
comprehensive 70
conciseness 61
consistency 107
contents 32-33
cover 32, 100

D

dash 33, 80, 82
data, types of
    primary 41
    secondary 41
diagonal 81

E

editing 106
    consistency 107
    style 106
    substance 106
ellipsis 47, 81, 117
e-mail 25
emphasis 69
endnotes 52, 118
evaluation report 24
exclamation point 81-82
executive summary/abstract 31
expletives 67
extra phrases 62

F

feasibility study 22
follow-up report 24
font alignment 94
fonts 89

footnotes 52, 118
form 26
format styles 25

G

graphics
   chart (graph) 100-102
   icons (symbols) 100
   logos 100
   photograph 101

H

headers and footers 99
headings and subheadings 98
hyphen 81-82, 125

I

implied ideas 61
inform 18
interpret 18
introduction 33
irrelevant information 61
italics 77

L

layout 96
leaders 33
line spacing 94

M

magazine 28
margins 97

N

newsletter 27, 29
numbers 77

O

objectives 38
objectivity 60
organization 17

outline 42
overall plan 40

P

page numbers 99
page orientation 97
paper 95
paraphrasing 48
parenthetical 51, 118
parentheses 51, 82, 108, 118, 129
period 82
persuade 19
plagiarism 54-56
positive vs. negative 66
press release 25
primary data 41
pronouns 67
proofreading 107-109
punctuation 79
punctuation marks
   apostrophe 79
   colon 79-80, 82
   comma 52, 65, 80, 82-83
   dash 33, 80, 82
   diagonal 81
   ellipsis points 47, 117
   exclamation points 81-82
   hyphen 81-82, 125
   parentheses 51, 82, 108, 118, 129
   period 82
   question mark 82
   quotation marks 47-48, 54, 82-83,
      108, 117, 119, 129
   semicolon 65, 82-83
   underscore 93, 124
purposes of reports 18
   inform 18
   interpret 18
   persuade 19
   recommend 19

Q

question mark 82
quotation marks 47-48, 54, 82-83, 108,
   117, 119, 129

R

recommend 19
redundancy 61
reference checkers 51
reference management software 49
repetition 64
reports, parts of
   appendix 34
   bibliography 34
   body 33
   contents 32
   executive summary 31
   introduction 33
   title page 32
research reports, types 20
   assessment 24
   business plan 23
   business proposal 23
   case study 21
   case study analysis 20
   evaluation 24
   feasibility study 22
   follow-up 24
   press release 24
   research 20
   synthesis 24
   technical 24
researching 41

S

secondary data 41
semicolon 65, 82-83
social media 29
sources
   primary 41
   secondary 41
spelling 83, 85, 108, 129
stereotyping 68
strategic plan 22
style 106
substance 106
summaries 48
synthesis report 24

T

target audience 39
technical report 24
text size 93
time schedule 39
tone 66
transition words 64

U

using style manuals 53

V

varietey 69

W

word division 85
writing style 59
writing style techniques
   coherence 64
   comprehensiveness 70
   conciseness 61
   emphasis 69
   objectivity 60
   tone 66
   variety 69

Edwards Brothers Malloy
Ann Arbor MI. USA
July 12, 2017